Spirals from the sea

Overleaf:

DECORATED SKULL, NEW GUINEA

The row of Ring Cowrie shells on this decorated Chambri skull from New Guinea indicates that this man was important and wealthy (see page 93).

SPIRALS FROM THE SEA

An anthropological look at shells

JANE FEARER SAFER AND FRANCES McLAUGHLIN GILL

DESIGNED BY BETTY BINNS

Clarkson N. Potter, Inc./Publishers   New York

PUBLISHED IN ASSOCIATION WITH THE AMERICAN MUSEUM OF NATURAL HISTORY

DISTRIBUTED BY CROWN PUBLISHERS, INC.

For my parents, for Morley, and for Sarah

Photographs © 1982 by Frances McLaughlin Gill

DESIGN: BETTY BINNS GRAPHICS/BETTY BINNS

LIBRARY OF CONGRESS CATALOGING IN PUBLICATION DATA

Safer, Jane.
  Spirals from the sea.

Bibliography: p.
Includes index.
1. Shells—Social aspects. 2. Shellcraft.
3. Shells (in religion, folklore, etc.)
I. Title.
GN435.7.S23   1981   390'.028   80-25923
ISBN: 0-517-540363

10 9 8 7 6 5 4 3 2 1
FIRST EDITION

CLARKSON N. POTTER, INC. *One Park Avenue New York, New York 10016*

Contents

ACKNOWLEDGMENTS

This book would not have been possible without the help of many people. My thanks to Mrs. Donald Newhouse, Mrs. Lily Auchincloss, and Mr. Joseph Fearer for their financial support, which made possible the acquisition of the photographs without which there would have been no book. To Dr. Thomas Nicholson, director of the American Museum of Natural History, and to David Ryus, vice-president, for their support and encouragement all along the way. To Mrs. Gardner Stout, who was responsible for the original concept of the Hall of Mollusks and Mankind, for her help. To Dr. Stanley Freed, chairman of the department of anthropology during the four years the exhibition was being prepared, for his generosity in sharing his experience and knowledge and for his patient tolerance. The research and preparation of the exhibition was a shared effort. Special thanks to Priscilla Ward, Judy Eisenberg, and Laila Williamson who worked on both the research and the exhibition; they are responsible for tracking down and interpreting the significance of much of the data included in this volume. Thanks also to the many volunteers who participated at various times in the research efforts, to members of the anthropology department who helped prepare the exhibition, and to those in the exhibition department—especially Henry Gardiner, Lee Drogin, and Peggy Cooper—who transformed our work into a beautiful permanent Hall.

Thanks to all those of the department of anthropology of the American Museum who contributed both to the exhibit and this book by giving unstintingly of their time and expertise: Junius Bird, Gordon Ekholm, Robert Carneiro, Craig Morris, David Hurst Thomas, Enid Schildkrout, the late Margaret Mead, Rhoda Metraux, Carin Burrows, Lisa Whittall, Betty Erda, and especially Phillip Gifford, whom we pestered more than anyone else in the department. Thanks to William Emerson, of the department of invertebrates, who had overall responsibility for the Hall of Mollusks and Mankind and bore the brunt of everyone's problems. To Dr. Emerson and other members of the department of invertebrates—William Olds, Harold Feinberg, Sidney Horenstein—who patiently made available their expertise in molluscan biology and classification of shells.

Many scholars outside the American Museum generously shared unpublished information. I would particularly like to thank Robert Tonkinson, Michiko Takaki, Sonam Paljor Densongpa, Richard Leavitt, Arthur Miller, Tang Mei-Chun, Schuyler Jones, Charles Hunt, Andrew and Marilyn Strathern, Richard Gould, Harold Ross, Robin Hide, Pascal Imperato, Deborah Gewertz, Dorothy Billings, Mr. Korwa, Mary Douglas, Nabuko Kajatani, Barrie Reynolds, Rabbi Chaim Gold, and many others.

For providing photographs I would like to thank Stella Snead, Harold Ross, Andrew and Marilyn Strathern, A. L. Epstein, and the late Margaret Mead.

I thank my husband and daughter for their forbearance and patience throughout this project. My thanks also to Frances McLaughlin Gill, not only for her superb photographs but also for always being there to push, or support, or whatever was necessary. To Patsy Barnes who brought Franny Gill, Jane West, and me together in the first place. To my editor, Carol Southern, who deserves a great deal of credit for whatever merits this book may have. To Betty Binns for designing a beautiful book. To Carolyn Hart of Clarkson Potter and to Anne-Marie Cunningham for their criticism and improvements of the text.

And especially to Jane West, my friend, my first editor, publisher of Clarkson Potter, without whose enthusiasm and continued support this book would never have happened. She is deeply missed by all of us who knew and loved her.

JANE FEARER SAFER
New York, 1982

Foreword

In the early 1970s the American Museum of Natural History's famed Hall of Mollusks and Mankind went from the drawing boards into construction. It was a daring plan for an institution philosophically grounded in the view that anthropology and malacology are essentially different disciplines, but we were convinced that such an exhibition was quite within our competence. We encouraged and nurtured the plan and built the hall with enthusiasm and imaginativeness.

So it was that in December of 1975 the Hall of Mollusks and Mankind emerged, a testament to the cross-disciplinary potentials of the American Museum and its staff. Our anthropologists and invertebrate biologists worked closely, researching, choosing, culling, labeling, and designing this jewel of an exhibition that tells our visitors—laymen, students, and scientists—about mollusks and how they have influenced human behavior, serving as instruments of many of man's activities. Mollusks have literally nourished mankind physically as well as spiritually.

Jane Fearer Safer's research for the hall was carried forward with the scholarly zeal of the anthropologist. As her writing attests, she was moved not only to discover but to explain what she learned about humankind through the mollusk and to help her readers interpret the meaning of her findings and seek new meanings through her work.

Our Hall of Mollusks does that for our visitors; since it opened, millions have passed through to study, to savor and enjoy, to be stimulated and amazed. Jane Safer gives the subject matter a quantum thrust outward to other constituencies who have not been able to visit our museum to see for themselves how mollusks and mankind relate. Mrs. Safer has brought the subject to them so that they, too, may study, savor, enjoy, be stimulated and amazed.

That this volume will serve as an important contribution to the body of knowledge on the subject, I have no doubt. That it has flowed from a project embodying the research, education, and exhibition capabilities of this museum reinforced our 112-year-old mission and does us proud.

THOMAS D. NICHOLSON, DIRECTOR
American Museum of Natural History

Introduction

A SOUTH AMERICAN native priest once said, "You can look at a tree and see a tree, or you can look at a tree and see a snake." By such imaginative leaps, human beings can transform shells—or any common natural object—into ritual objects, symbols, metaphors. The shell becomes a hiding place, the sun, a womb. In our contemporary experience, we mainly find this kind of metaphorical thinking in poetry. From European literature come images of the shell as a natural fortress, a grave, an image of resurrection, a toothed vagina—a small sample of the range of analogies that the human mind can imagine. This book attempts to understand the ideas that different peoples of the world have imaginatively linked to shells. The book grew out of research for the Hall of Mollusks and Mankind at the American Museum of Natural History in New York City. In a unique departure from conventional museum practice, this hall presents not only shells themselves but the biology of mollusks (the creatures that live inside shells), and the human uses of both mollusks and their shells. To my knowledge, this project was the first such attempt at collaboration between anthropologists and natural scientists.

In planning the exhibition, my colleagues and I in the anthropology department decided against what might have been the simplest presentation—a display of shell artifacts from different regions of the world—because we felt this sort of exhibit, while visually attractive, would be intellectually insubstantial. What we wanted to do was to examine not only how people have used shells but how they have thought about them. What we found particularly interesting was the wide range of symbolic meanings that shells have had for various peoples: as ritual objects, as signs of wealth, as emblems of kings and warriors. Shells are found throughout the world; we wanted to look at how peoples have perceived shells differently and have endowed these common natural objects with totally different kinds of meaning.

Our first step in preparing the exhibit was a search through dozens of museum storerooms jammed with objects of every description to find artifacts made entirely or partly from shells. We soon found ourselves overwhelmed by hundreds of objects ranging from hats and necklaces to fishhooks and war shields. The next problem was how to deal with this mass of material. Sociocultural anthropologists have not developed any general theories about the relationship of animals or other natural phenomena to human society that could provide us with an intellectual framework or at least a starting point. We elected to research thoroughly, region by region, each potentially interesting shell artifact, in the belief that organizing principles would eventually emerge out of the objects themselves.

We soon discovered that we would not find any quick and direct answers in books. Anthropologists have rarely shown much interest in the significance of shells except when shells were so important to the people themselves— as in New Guinea and Australia—that they could not avoid doing so. For the most part, looking up the meaning of artifacts in any book was useless; shells were rarely even mentioned in the index. In deciphering the significance of an object within its own society, social and cultural anthropologists generally rely on their own powers of observation and on native informants, alternatives obviously not available to us. We had to start from the objects, like archaeologists, who have long been accustomed to extracting information about a people from things they have owned or made. We began to think of the museum's storerooms as a vast archaeological site. We asked questions about the artifacts that have usually been asked only by anthropologists in the field. When we began, we really did not believe that we would be able to answer even the most basic questions—who used this object, how, and on what occasions—much less why one particular shell was used or what it meant to those who used it. To our surprise, we *were* able to piece together this information in a large number of cases. A major impetus behind this book was the publishing of these findings and the presentation of some of the hypotheses and speculations that resulted from looking at museum artifacts in a new way.

The enormous amount of detective work involved in tracking down answers to our questions led us into unexpected areas. Since few modern anthropologists appear ever to have asked their informants about the significance of shells, our best sources frequently were nineteenth- and early twentieth-century works by missionaries, travelers, explorers, historians, and anthropologists, who had haphazardly asked their informants about everything, meticulously recorded the answers, and so, inadvertently, included information on shells.

In order to consider any artifact for inclusion in the exhibit, we had to determine where the object came from, what shells it was made of, how it was used, under what circumstances, and by whom. If we were lucky, we might discover all this information in the catalogs of the museum collections. At other times a catalog entry might be as uninformative as "dance skirt, Africa." Sometimes the catalog was not merely uninformative but actually misleading. The entry "fetish, Baluba, Chimbundu, Kasai region, Congo" led us on a lengthy and fruitless search for a place or people called Chimbundu. Much later we accidentally stumbled on a book of photographs taken by the collector of the fetish, Frederick Starr, including an account of his expedition and a rough map. We finally determined that the object came from the Lulua people, not the Baluba, and that Chimbundu was not a subtribe, a village, or a river. It was, in fact, the name of the man who was chief of the village when Starr passed through in 1905.

Gradually, starting from the artifacts themselves and proceeding with whatever information was available in catalogs and field notes, published books and articles, and consultations with specialists, we were able to piece together information about many artifacts. It was rather like doing a jigsaw puzzle with many pieces missing, always hoping for that exciting moment when we could either fit together enough pieces to see what the picture was or find a key piece that would make all the others fall into place. This research process led us to interesting speculative interpretations and some unexpected conclusions.

In the course of trying to discover the meaning of the shells in each society, we found that certain themes did emerge. The first theme focused on shell artifacts as part of a visual language. When people of a particular group wear a certain shell, usually they are communicating to all those who see it—and understand its meaning—something about the wearer and his place in society. These shells form part of a visual system of communication; our task was to decipher the symbols—to break the code—in order to discover precisely what was being communicated.

The second theme was the linkage between shells and ideas. We focused on how people think about shells: the process by which they endow a common natural object with meaning or transform it into a symbol. We tried to discover what ideas about a shell made it appropriate for a particular meaning or how qualities of a shell, such as its color or shape, related to other aspects of a belief system.

A question that may occur to the reader is to what extent the practices described here are still going on. When there is a high degree of certainty either that a practice is current or that it has died out, this is indicated in the text. When the "ethnographic present" tense is used, it means that the information is fairly recent, but whether the behavior continues in precisely the same form is difficult to know; in some cases, rituals have appeared to die out only to be revitalized decades later. The term *in modern times* is used to denote conditions that have been true during the twentieth century and may or may not still be true.

Among the chapters that follow, the first will concentrate on the utilitarian uses human beings have found for many parts of the mollusk. Subsequent chapters focus on how people think about shells: first, as wealth; second, as visual signs of status; and third, as elements in ritual and myth. I shall present information we unearthed and hypotheses we developed, but I hope that I shall also be able to communicate some of the excitement of this process of discovery.

JANE FEARER SAFER
New York City

Spirals from the sea

WOMEN IN INDIA GATHERING COCKLES

Shells in daily life

Wʜᴀᴛ is a shell and where does it come from? Although clams, oysters, and snails are commonly known throughout the world, the word *mollusk,* which scientists use to classify them in the animal world, is less familiar. All mollusks are invertebrates, animals without backbones. The word is derived from the Latin word *mollis,* which means "soft." All mollusks have a soft body, a slippery skin, and a fleshy covering lobe or pair of lobes, known as the mantle, and most have shells that protect their soft, vulnerable bodies.* Shells come in many sizes and shapes, but in embryonic form all shells are spirals.

Fifty thousand to eighty thousand species of mol-

*However, not all mollusks have shells. Octopus, squid, or the common garden slug have either vestigial shells deep within their bodies or no shells at all. Conversely, not all animals with shells are mollusks: Crabs, barnacles, lobster, shrimp, and sand dollars belong to other major groups.

lusk inhabit an extraordinary range of habitats, from the coldest climate to the warmest, from ocean floors to mountain heights. Most species live in the sea, some in fresh water, and some even on land.

Of the seven major classes of mollusks, humans most frequently make use of gastropods and bivalves.* Gastropods, which include cowries, conchs, and land snails, form the largest class. All have single coiled or cap-shaped shells. About half of this class, collectively known as sea snails, live in oceans. Bivalves (oysters, clams, scallops, cockles, mussels) have uncoiled, wedge-shaped shells with two halves hinged at the top edge attached by a ligament. All bivalves are aquatic; about two-thirds live in salt water.

All mollusks follow the same fundamental body plan. The upper body mass, or visceral lump, contains most of the organs of reproduction, circulation, digestion, and excretion. The lower part of the body, which can be extended from the shell, consists of two distinct regions: the head for feeding and sensing the environment and the foot for moving about. Unique to mollusks is the mantle, which secretes the shell. The mantle also encloses the respiratory organs—either gills or lungs—and contains the organs of taste and smell. The shell is also formed by the mantle, which as the animal grows and develops, slowly secretes the several distinct layers of the spiral form.

*Other classes are Aplacophora (wormlike mollusks with no shell), Polyplacophora (chitons with overlapping shelly plates), Monoplacophora (cap-shaped marine mollusks), Scaphopoda (tusk or tooth shells), and Cephalopoda (which include squid, octopus, and nautilus).

THE MOLLUSK AS FOOD

The flesh of almost all mollusks is edible, and most species have been part of the diet of one human group or another. Throughout most of human history mollusks have been an important source of protein. Many archaeologists believe that mollusks also played an important role in the evolution of human society. Huge prehistoric piles, called *middens,* of discarded shells have been found in coastal areas all over the world.

Before the last ice age, seven to eight thousand years ago, coastal waters were deep, but as glaciers melted, the level of the sea rose to cover the continental shelf. This change in water level created shallow coastal waters, a hospitable environment for many species of mollusks. Clams burrowed in the sand in shallow water; oysters and mussels clung to rocks. Unlike game animals, most mollusks do not migrate from one place to another, or appear only briefly in season, like wild nuts and fruits. Early peoples could easily collect substantial quantities of mollusks with the simplest technology: They needed only their hands or a stick to dig mollusks out of the sand or to pry them off rocks.

For the first time in history people had a source of protein that was reliable the year round. They no longer had to keep moving after game or wild plants. Until recently most archaeologists thought that people did not settle down into sedentary communities until after the development of agriculture. We now know that the

INDIAN WOMAN GATHERING MUSSELS, BRITISH COLUMBIA

availability of mollusks as a dependable food source enabled some coastal peoples to abandon nomadic ways and establish settled communities even before they developed agriculture.

People have been cultivating mollusks for over two thousand years. The ancient Chinese and Romans practiced oyster cultivation, which still remains an important industry in modern countries like Japan, France, and the United States. Land snails have been farmed in the Middle East since ancient times, as they still are today in France. Africans today are attempting to farm a dietary staple, the Giant African Land Snail.

The species of mollusks considered edible varies widely from one culture to another. Many North Americans relish the idea of a clambake or Oysters Rockefeller but shrink from the thought of eating land snails, a delicacy to many Frenchmen, or the shell-less land snails known as garden slugs, which the Japanese enjoy. The Ashanti of Ghana define themselves as a people partly by the fact that they eat land snails, a preference that distinguishes them from the people of northern Ghana, who consider land snails inedible. Whether a mollusk is considered edible is a purely cultural matter and has little to do with any of the animal's inherent properties.

In the West, from the time of ancient Rome until the nineteenth century, mollusks were a staple food of the urban poor. Fuel was scarce and overcrowding in highly flammable buildings made cooking fires dangerous as well as expensive. Unable to cook at home, tenement dwellers bought hot food at cookshops and depended on foods that did not require cooking, like oysters, clams, mussels, and cockles.

Folk song has perpetuated the street vendor's famous cry: "Cockles and mussels, alive, alive-O." In 1864 a half-billion tons of oysters were sold at London's Billingsgate market alone. As one of Dickens's characters remarked in *Pickwick Papers,* published in 1837, "Poverty and oysters always seem to go together. The poorer a place is, the greater call there seems to be for oysters." But in the second half of the nineteenth century, urban centers like London and New York, rapidly swelling with immigrants, disastrously depleted local oyster beds in less than two decades. In New York State oyster beds that had extended far up the Hudson River disappeared completely. By the late 1880s, on both sides of the Atlantic, only the wealthy could afford oysters. After nearly two thousand years as a symbol of poverty, oysters had become a luxury.

SHELLS IN ARCHAEOLOGY

The fact that coastal people all over the world have been eating shellfish since ancient times and leaving heaps of shells behind has provided archaeologists with invaluable information, for shells, unlike many tools, utensils, and fabric, do not disintegrate. These prehistoric shell dumps are called shell middens. They may be hundreds of feet deep and wide, made up mainly of shells that a people discarded after eating the soft animals inside.

These ancient heaps found in coastal areas all over the world—Japan, California, Chile, the North American Atlantic Coast, Scandinavia—can reveal a great deal about the life, environment, and behavior of ancient peoples. Throughout the four thousand years during which people repeatedly settled and abandoned the midden shown here, the species of shell most common in the midden varied as food preferences changed. Although oysters *(Crassostrea gigas)* would have been available throughout the entire four thousand years, they predominate in the midden's upper layers, of more recent date. But in the lower layers of earlier times, no oysters are found. Clams *(Meretrix meretrix),* however, are present in small quantities throughout all the shell layers. Six thousand years later, clams remain a popular food in Japan.

Besides food preferences, changes in species from a midden's earliest layer at the bottom to the later levels at the top also reveal changes in climate and geography. Many mollusks cannot tolerate changes in water temperature, salinity, or depth; therefore, variations in the dominant species in a midden may accurately reflect changes in the environment. In the earlier, lower layers of the model midden, warm-water clams *(Anadara granosa)* are most abundant. In later levels, a cold-water scallop *(Pecten yesoensis)* predominates, indicating that the water temperature had become colder in the later era.

A change in shells can indicate shifts in geography as well as climate. In the middle layers of the model midden are marine snails *(Rapana venosa* and *Batillaria multiformis),*

Facing page:

MODEL OF A JAPANESE
SHELL MIDDEN

This model depicting a cross section of a shell midden is a composite of middens found in Japan in the Kanto Plain east of Tokyo Bay. This site was inhabited intermittently for over four thousand years, from 4500 B.C. to 500 B.C. Two layers of sterile earth containing no remnants of human occupation indicate intervals of hundreds of years when the site was temporarily abandoned. Although the sterile layers are relatively narrow, they represent longer periods of time than the shell layers, since earth layers build up much more slowly. The ash layer represents the remains of an ancient fire pit.

which breed in shallow salt water, while in the uppermost layer a freshwater clam *(Corbicula leaena)* is most common. This change suggests that in its earliest eras this midden lay by the sea, or more likely by a saltwater inlet, but by 250 B.C. the ocean had receded and the saltwater inlet had turned into a freshwater lake—a common occurrence at sites on the Kanto plain. Using geological and fossil clues, as well as artifacts such as pottery of known dates that appear associated with freshwater or saltwater mollusks, archaeologists can plot changes in the coastline over time.

The shell middens also provide information by preserving physical evidence and cultural artifacts. The calcium carbonate (lime) content of the shells neutralizes acid in soil and inhibits decay of organic materials, especially bone. Thus, the model midden contains animal bones, stone tools, and pieces of pottery. Nearly all the human bones we have from ancient Japan are the remains of people who were buried in shell middens. These bones are our sole evidence of the ancient population's physical characteristics and state of health. Preserved animal bones tell us what game people hunted and ate. The kinds of shell, bone, and stone tools found in middens offer clues to early methods of hunting, fishing, and food preparation. The style of the pottery found in a midden can be used to date the layer where it was found.

Shell middens played an important role in the intellectual breakthrough that occurred in the infant science of archaeology in the mid-nineteenth century. Previously, archaeologists had concerned themselves solely

MODEL OF A JAPANESE
SHELL MIDDEN

with the architecture and religion of literate peoples. The realization that by investigating garbage heaps researchers could learn about the daily lives of peoples who left no records opened the door to study of prehistoric peoples.

Archaeologists made intensive studies of shell middens in the second half of the nineteenth century, but by 1900 scholarly interest had turned to pottery styles and stone-chipping techniques. Recently, new technologies and a change in the kinds of questions archaeologists ask have combined to make shells once again of great interest.

Modern archaeologists try to answer questions about such subjects as a people's residence patterns, ecology, or social and political organization, as well as the traditional questions of dating, chronology, or subsistence. Thanks to advances in geology, paleontology, chemistry, and other natural sciences, shells can help answer some of these questions. Carbon-14 dating can determine the age of a shell with reasonable accuracy. Measuring oxygen isotopes in the shell can reveal the temperature of the water when the mollusk was collected, showing changes in climate or, if the climate was similar to today's, indicating at what season of the year the mollusk was caught. Another relatively new technique that has proved fruitful is the analysis of a shell's microscopic growth rings. The shell is formed by the mantle, which slowly secretes the several distinct layers of the spiral form. Microscopic examination of the shell's surface reveals fine growth lines, reflecting a cyclical pattern of seasonal or even daily growth. Archaeologists find these lines useful because irregularities in their spacing, size, or color reflect changes in salinity, temperature, light, and diet.

If the shells in a midden are of a species still found in the region, the patterns can be studied and applied to excavated shells. For example, if dark rings are formed every December, the archaeologist can count the rings between the last dark ring and the last growth ring at the edge of the shell to determine the season or even the month the mollusk was collected. Shells collected evenly throughout the year suggest a settled people. Shells from only certain seasons would suggest either a nomadic people who made a regular stop at a site or a settled people who relied on mollusks only when other food was scarce.

Land snails, found almost everywhere, are an even more sensitive indicator of changes in humidity, temperature, vegetation, and soil. Most land snails cannot survive outside a narrow range of environmental conditions. Therefore, the shell remains of land snails can provide very specific information about climate, soil, and vegetation at a site at a particular time, as well as a record of changes over time. In a site that had been cultivated fields, the snails would differ from those in a bordering uncultivated area around dwellings. A change in the amount of rainfall would be reflected by a change in the snail species. Different snails found at various levels of a site could indicate when a field was abandoned or planted.

Besides providing clues to changes in environmental conditions, shells enable archaeologists to trace trade routes. Shells are among the earliest trade objects known to archaeologists. The presence of Indo-Pacific shells in prehistoric caves in Britain and France means that as early as Neolithic times trade networks stretched from western Europe to Asia. Because biologists usually know shells' native habitats, specific trade routes can frequently be plotted from one shell's place of origin to archaeological sites hundreds or even thousands of miles away.

MOLLUSCAN PURPLE DYE

Within the body of some mollusks a gland secretes a fluid that produces one of the world's rarest and most valuable dyes, shellfish purple. Best known as the royal or Tyrian purple of antiquity, shellfish purple was also known to ancient Peruvians and is still used as dye in Mexico, Guatemala, and Japan. When the mollusk is disturbed, it retreats into its shell and ejects the fluid, which initially is colorless but, once exposed to sunlight, gradually turns from yellow to green to blue and finally to a purplish red. The precise function this secretion serves is unclear, but it probably protects the mollusk or its eggs from predators.

In antiquity, shellfish dye was of great economic importance around the Mediterranean. The most desirable dyes were produced in the Phoenician cities of Tyre and Sidon, and contributed substantially to Phoenicia's pre-eminence in trade. The flowering of the Mediterranean dye industry coincided with the height of the silk trade with China. The Romans wanted Chinese silk, and purple-dyed

PRE-COLUMBIAN SHELL MASK, ARKANSAS (USA)

Shells were among the first items whose origin scholars could pinpoint, and shells found in sites far from their native habitats reveal the extent of ancient trade networks. The Hopewell culture, which flourished from 200 B.C. to A.D. 500, had its center in Ohio, but archaeologists have been able to trace silver, copper, gold, and shell found in Hopewell sites to origins as far away as Yellowstone, Montana, and southern Florida. This mask, probably made from lightning Whelk (Busycon contrarium), was found in the Saint Francis Valley, Arkansas, several hundred miles from the sea.

fabrics were one of the few goods that the Chinese were willing to accept in exchange.

As early as the seventeenth century B.C., Phoenicians had developed techniques for extracting the dye. Dyers crushed the smaller dye mollusks (the Red-mouthed Rock shell, *Thais haemastoma* and *Murex trunculus)*, shell and all. The larger Dye Murex *(M. brandaris)* was carefully opened to remove the dye gland whole. Mixed with salt and water, this mass simmered in lead cauldrons for about ten days, after which raw wool was soaked in the still-clear liquid which turned purplish red when exposed to sunlight. Depending on the species of mollusk, the final product varied from red to violet to almost black. Enormous quantities of mollusks were necessary to produce a tiny amount of dye: Twelve thousand specimens of the larger Dye Murex produced a mere 1.5 grams of pure dye.

From earliest recorded time, the use of purple dye was restricted to individuals of the highest rank. Throughout the ancient Mediterranean, purple dye became an emblem of sovereignty, a meaning that has survived to the present day in phrases like "born to the purple." In ancient Israel, the robes of the high priest of the temple of Jerusalem were dyed with molluscan purple. The ancient Greeks envisioned their gods as dressed in purple, and they reserved the color for the greatest statesmen and artists. In Rome, Julius and Augustus Caesar permitted only themselves and their highest officials to wear robes with purple stripes. In the third century A.D. the manufacture of purple dye became a monopoly of the Roman state. Purple gradually became a decorative element rather than a special privilege.

The Old Testament distinguishes two colors of molluscan dye: "red" and "blue." The "blue" was so rare that it could be collected only every seventy years and was used to dye just one thread at each corner of the prayer shawl worn by devout Jews. Recent research has discovered the source to be a very rare mollusk, the Violet Snail, *Janthina janthina,* which is bluish purple in color and floats on the surface of open sea. On rare occasions severe storms might blow them toward the coast, where fishermen could gather them in nets.

In the North Atlantic a Dog Whelk, *Nucella lapillus,* was another source of purple dye. Irish shell middens consisting almost entirely of Dog Whelks are evidence of a European dye industry dating back to 1000 B.C. In the Middle Ages monks used purple parchment for their most important illuminated manuscripts, lettered in silver and gold. In Ireland monks dyed the parchment with Dog Whelk; on the Continent, with Tyrian purple.

In Asia molluscan purple was known but not widely used. Some sources say that the emperor of Japan wore robes dyed with molluscan purple; in medieval Japan purple was considered the most perfect color and was restricted to the emperor. Several plants in Japan produce an intense purple dye, and there is no evidence to suggest any ancient use of shellfish dye in Japan. However, in modern times Japanese fishermen use it to mark their clothing; since the markings do not fade, they identify the drowned. *Thais clavigera, T. luteostoma,* and *Rapana venosa* are the mollusks used for this purple.

LIME CONTAINER, PHILIPPINES

Throughout the Pacific Islands and in parts of Asia, betel nuts are commonly chewed. The betel nut, like the coca leaf, contains an alkaloid whose narcotic effect is activated when chewed with shell lime. The Hanunoo people of the Philippines carry shell lime in containers like this one, made from a Lettered Cone shell (Conus litteratus).

In the Western Hemisphere molluscan purple dye has been found on fabrics from the Paracas and Ica valleys of Peru (400–100 B.C.), probably from *Concholepas concholepas*. Today, Indians along Mexico's Pacific coast use dye from the Wide-mouthed Purpura *(Purpura patula pansa).* Even though yarns dyed with aniline dyes are available at a fraction of the cost, these Indians still prefer genuine shellfish dye for clothing worn on special occasions.

SHELL LIME

A fully formed mollusk shell consists of layers of lime in the crystalline form of argonite or, less commonly, calcite. Since prehistory, humans have obtained this chemical lime—an important plant nutrient and a building material essential to cement and plaster—by simply pulverizing shells. In New England, Indians taught early settlers to improve the soil by adding crushed shells. About forty-five hundred years ago, people began to burn shells to make slaked lime, which became the first manufactured chemical. Modern industrial societies still use lime for fertilizer and construction, although the source is more apt to be limestone than shells. Nevertheless, for many coastal peoples, shells remain a major source of lime. Shell lime is widely used as temper in pottery, to prevent shrinkage and cracking during firing. Since shell temper is easily detected, it enables archaeologists to pinpoint where the piece of pottery was made and to trace trade contacts.

Throughout the Pacific shell lime is used as paint on wooden figures and masks. In other parts of the world, shell is also used as an ingredient in glue and caulking

SOUTH AMERICAN INDIAN CHEWING COCA
AND POWDERED LIME

Dipping a stick into his gourd container, this Saha Indian of the Colombian Andes adds powdered shell lime to the wad of coca leaves he is chewing. In pre-Columbian times lime containers were made of many materials, including shells encrusted with gold; today they are usually gourds.

mixtures. The Tlingit of southern Alaska glued seams of wooden boxes with a paste of burned clamshells, seal blood, seal oil, and salmon eggs. Around the Red Sea, a mixture of shells and shark oil is still used to caulk boats.

Throughout the Andes mountains of South America, Indians use shell lime to extract the narcotic from coca leaves. Indians claim that chewing coca helps them overcome hunger and cold, enabling them to work longer and harder in the high altitude and cold of the high Andes. Recent research suggests that when the lime reacts with the coca leaves not only is the narcotic activated but a new chemical formed that helps the body adapt to these stresses.

North American Indians used to mix equal quantities of powdered tobacco and burned river shells. They claimed that, during desert travel, sucking on small balls of this mixture would prevent hunger and thirst over several days. Researchers have yet to investigate the effect of lime on the narcotic properties of tobacco.

SHELLS AS CONTAINERS, TOOLS, AND UTENSILS

It has been the shell of the mollusk that people have found most useful in their daily lives. The natural shape of many shells suits them for use as containers and tools, with little or no alteration. The rounded, hollow shape of shells, like the larger bivalves or the nautilus shell, readily converts into bowls, cups, or spoons. Spoons made from shell have

RASP AND AUGER, PACIFIC ISLANDS

Above: People of Manus Island in the Admiralty Islands, Bismarck Archipelago, used this spindle shell (Fuscinus undata) as a boring tool. Right: On New Caledonia, Melanesia, an ark shell (Anadara granosa) lashed to a wooden handle became a rasp.

HIGHLAND NEW GUINEA MAN HOLDING SHELL AX

been found in every continent. Although these uses of shells are most common among coastal peoples, inland dwellers have frequently employed freshwater shells for spoons, bowls, or knives. Shell spoons have not been limited to simple societies; seventeenth- and eighteenth-century European craftsmen attached silver handles to rare and beautiful shells.

Oil lamps made of shells are frequent archaeological finds throughout the Middle East. A four-thousand-year-old Sumerian lamp found at Ur was made from a Spider Conch (*Lambis* sp.) imported all the way from the Indian Ocean. Later oil lamps of clay, silver, and gold imitated the form of these early shell lamps. The modern Balinese make similar lamps from Bear's Paw shell (*Hippopus hippopus*) in which a burning wick floats in oil.

Shells have been decorative and useful, but only on the coral islands of the Pacific and Caribbean have they been crucial to subsistence. Coral islands have no stone; shell is the only raw material locally available for the manufacture of tools and weapons. In the Pacific, the Giant Clam shell (*Tridacna gigas*), which can grow as large as four feet across and is as hard and durable as stone, has been the primary material for making heavy tools and weapons. In the Caribbean and parts of Florida, the pre-Columbian inhabitants used Queen Conch shell (*Strombus gigas*) for gouges, axes, and weapons.

Unlike the rest of the world, where the role of shells in

GIANT CLAM SHELL

One of the largest specimens of Giant Clam shell ever collected—measuring four and one-half feet across, owned by the American Museum of Natural History.

CUTTING GIANT CLAM SHELL, NEW GUINEA

DRILLING GIANT CLAM SHELL, NEW GUINEA

WORKING GIANT CLAM SHELL, NEW GUINEA

Giant Clam shell is extremely difficult to work, and only a few specially skilled craftsmen know the manufacturing techniques. The New Guinea men shown far left have roughly hacked the huge shell—as large as four feet across—into smaller workable pieces, fastened a chunk of shell into a frame, and are proceeding to saw it into flat plates. The plates will then be smoothed with braided bamboo fibers moistened with water and dipped into sand.

The photograph here shows a New Guinea man with a clamshell disc on a wooden plate bound with rattan to keep the drill from slipping. He drills the center hole with a large wooden staff whose base is embedded with extremely hard bamboo splinters. His final step will be to smooth the edges and polish the rings on an abrasive stone. A single large arm ring might require several months work.

subsistence is relatively minor, people on these coral islands tend to be extremely dependent on shells. On one coral island, Tuamotu, near Tahiti, Giant Clams are the inhabitants' main source of protein, supplemented by Pearl Oysters, clams, Green Turban snails, and octopus. Tuamotans prepare their food with pounders made of Giant Clam shell, scrape meat out of coconuts with shell scrapers, cut their food with shell knives, and dig up taro root with spades made of large Black-lipped Pearl Oyster shells *(Pinctada margaritifera)*. The adzes and axes they need for clearing land to plant food crops or to cut down trees to build houses are made of Giant Clam shell. They fashion chisels for fine woodworking from the outer lip of a Bull-mouth Helmet shell *(Cypraecassis rufa)* and fishhooks from pearl shell. A shell tool splits and smooths pandanus leaves for thatching roofs and making baskets and mats. Turtle shell and imported stone or wood may also be used to make tools and utensils, but these materials are harder to obtain. Shell objects are essential to most households on Tuamotu, as on most coral islands in the Pacific and the pre-Columbian Caribbean.

SHELL COLOR AND PATTERN

Because of the extraordinary variety of shells' surface colors and patterns, they have been used throughout the world for their decorative qualities. The shell mantle, which secretes the shell layers, also forms the surface ornament and coloration. Tropical shells, in particular, often have surface patterns in brilliant shades of orange,

SHELL CUP, ANDAMAN ISLANDS

A woman from the Andaman Islands in the Indian Ocean feeds her baby from Nautilus shell (Nautilus pompilius).

purple, pink, or yellow. Color and pattern are largely genetically controlled, but they may vary in response to the mollusk's environment. Sometimes color depends on diet. For example, the red, brown, and green bands on the Japanese Abalone shell reflect the availability of red, brown, and green algae.

The mollusk's shell consists of one or more lime layers sandwiched between a protective outer layer and an inner limey layer. All embryonic shells have an outer protective layer called the *periostricum,* which some retain at maturity. In some species the periostricum is transparent, but in some snails and clams it is so dark that it completely hides the shell's color and pattern. The Akawaio Indians of Guyana in northeast South America make disc ornaments of land snail shell, decorated with what appears to be a design of brown paint. When we took these ornaments to our mollusk expert, we discovered that what we had taken to be paint was in fact an opaque periostricum, selectively scraped away to create a design against the pale shell layer beneath.

Other craftsmen have taken decorative advantage of differently colored shell layers. For hundreds of years Italian cameo-makers have sculpted faces and figures from the white outer layer of various helmet shells, while the brown, orange, or yellow inner layer serves as a contrasting background.

In some snails, like abalones, and in freshwater mussels and oysters, the inner layer may be composed of the lustrous, nacreous material unique to mollusks, known as mother-of-pearl. Since prehistoric times the iridescent inner layer of many shells, especially the Black-lipped Pearl Oyster shell *(Pinctada margaritifera)* has been widely used for ornament, inlay in particular. Pacific fishermen have also made pearl oyster shells into fishhooks, an equally ancient but less familiar use. The gleam of the pearl shell serves as a lure, eliminating the need for bait. Pearl Oyster fishhooks, nearly identical in shape to those still used by Solomon Islanders, have been found in shell middens in California and Chile dating from A.D. 100. Fishermen in the Solomons carve their iridescent fishhooks into beautiful tiny fish; Marshall Islanders use irregular chinks from the hinge section of the Pearl Oyster shell.

Besides the shell's several layers, most aquatic snails have an operculum, or "trapdoor," a horny or limey plate attached to the foot of the mollusk. When the snail withdraws into its shell, the operculum seals the opening, protecting the mollusk from its enemies. Most opercula are insignificant in size, but some, like the operculum of the Green Turban Snail *(Turbo marmoratus),* can measure three and a half inches in diameter. North American Pacific Coast Indians used opercula to represent eyes and teeth on masks and bowls.

For some species, shell color and pattern contribute to survival. The bright green of certain tree snails camouflages them among a tree's leaves. But in most species color and pattern do not seem to have any function and are frequently hidden. The cowrie shell's surface is obscured by its mantle, and the beautiful patterns of many cone shells are covered by a thick, opaque periostricum.

SPOONS, PHILIPPINES

These spoons or ladles were cut from baler shell (Melo sp.) in the Philippine Islands.

SHELL FISHHOOKS

These fishhooks made from pearl shell come from, clockwise, from the top: the Marshall Islands, Solomon Islands, Solomon Islands, California, and Cook Islands. All of these fishhooks are from the modern period except the California hook, which is of Pre-Columbian origin.

KNIFE, TWEEZERS, AND TWO SCRAPERS

With a little filing, the naturally sharp edges of many shells, especially bivalves, can be used as knives or scrapers.
Top right: Scraper from the Solomon Islands cut from pearl shell. Throughout the Pacific Islands scrapers made from a wide variety of shells are used for removing the meat from coconuts or breadfruit, cutting up taro, or extracting palm fiber.
Top left: The Shipibo people of Peru used the pair of freshwater river mussels (Castalia ambigua) as tweezers.
Center: Knives made from bivalves, like this freshwater clamshell from Angrifshafen, New Guinea, are common throughout the Pacific Islands.
Bottom: Northern California Indians hooked the California Mussel shell (Mytilus californiensis) over the thumb and scraped fiber from lily leaves to make twine.

BIRD-SHAPED WOODEN BOWL, SOLOMON ISLANDS

Mother-of-pearl—the lustrous, iridescent inner layer of shells like Black-lipped Pearl Oyster shell (Pinctada margaritifera) or Gold-lipped Pearl Oyster (P. maxima)—has been used decoratively in many parts of the world. This bird motif bowl and the one on the following page are separated in space by thousands of miles and in time by hundreds of years. This bird-shaped wooden bowl ornamented with pearl shell inlay was collected in the Solomon Islands in the nineteenth century. The Peruvian gourd bowl with pearl and stone inlay was found at Gran Chimu on the coast of Peru and dates from about A.D. 1200 to 1400.

DETAIL OF BIRD-SHAPED WOODEN BOWL, SOLOMON ISLANDS

DETAIL: PERUVIAN BOWL WITH SHELL INLAY

PERUVIAN BOWL WITH SHELL INLAY

Following page:

PRE-COLUMBIAN BAG AND PILLOW, PERU

Many peoples of the world have found that the bright orange of Pacific Thorny Oyster shell (Spondylus princeps) and Jewel Box shell (Chama sp.), or the purple rim of the Atlantic Quahog, or Hard-shell Clam (Mercenaria mercenaria) have provided a decorative and durable material for making beads. These two Peruvian objects made of networks of beads—a pillow and a bag for coca leaves (like the shell bib on page 83)—were found in a grave at Gran Chimu on the coast of Peru. All the orange beads are made from the shell of the Thorny Oyster. Because of the almost total absence of rain in Peru's coastal desert, the fiber stringing of the beads and the pillow's stuffing were found intact hundreds of years after they were made.

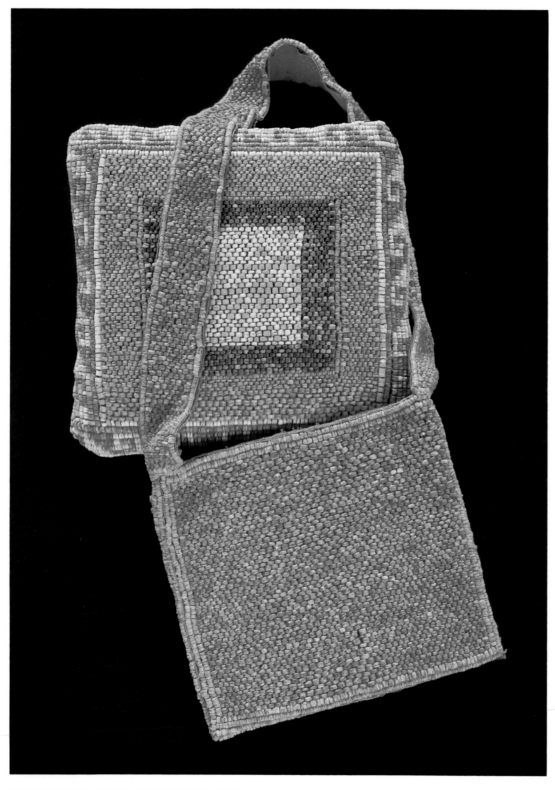

PRE-COLUMBIAN BAG AND PILLOW, PERU

DETAIL: PERUVIAN BAG AND PILLOW

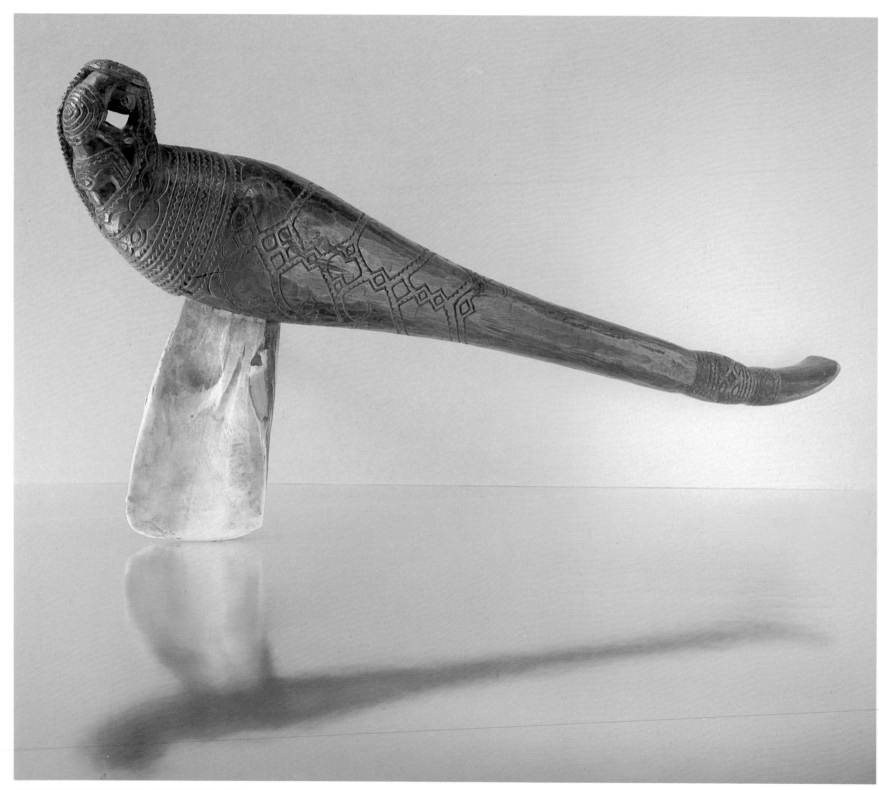

AX WITH SHELL BLADE, PACIFIC ISLANDS

HIGHLAND NEW GUINEA
MAN HOLDING SHELL AX

Facing page:

AX WITH SHELL BLADE, PACIFIC ISLANDS

*This ax was made by the
people of Kaniet Island,
Bismarck Archipelago,
near New Guinea. Its
head was cut from Giant
Clam shell and its wooden
handle has been carved in
the shape of a bird.*

OCTOPUS LURE, TAHITI

*In Tahiti and Hawaii fishermen used cowrie shell to
make octopus lures, like this lure of wood, Tiger
Cowrie (Cypraea tigris), Reticulated Cowrie (C.
maculifera) and C. ventriculus. The fisherman searches
the water for piles of discarded cowrie shells, the
octopus's favorite food. Then he lowers the lure to
attract the octopus. When the octopus emerges from its
hiding place and approaches the boat, the fisherman
hooks it and hauls it in.*

Shells as wealth

THROUGHOUT the world, the material most commonly used as a standard of value and as coin has been metal—primarily gold, silver, and occasionally iron. The second most common material has been shell. In the ancient world, shell money was used in areas around the Mediterranean, in Asia Minor, and in India; the Chinese paid taxes in cowrie shells. Seven hundred years ago West Africans traded gold for cowrie shells. More recently the Yurok Indians of northern California counted their wealth in tusk shells; the Pomo Indians of central California measured theirs in clamshell beads. In modern times shell money has circulated in Africa, Melanesia, India, Thailand, and North America. In fact the only major regions of the world where shells have never circulated as money are South America and Australia.

Facing page:

DETAIL: SHELL VALUABLES, NEW GUINEA

COWRIE SHELLS

No species of shell has traveled greater distances or in greater quantities than cowrie shells. Cowries, primarily the shiny yellow Money Cowrie *(Cypraea moneta)* and Ring Cowrie *(C. annulus)*, have circulated as currency in more places in the world than any coin. As academic economists love to point out, cowrie shells have all of money's necessary characteristics: They are uniform in shape and size; they are small, portable, and very durable. Furthermore, cowrie shells have one advantage over coins: They are almost impossible to counterfeit.

Even as early as 1200–800 B.C. cowrie shells were important valuables in China. Inscriptions on ancient bronzes record kings and princes rewarding honored nobles with cowrie shells. Han Dynasty documents (200 B.C.–A.D. 200) refer to cowries used as currency in ancient China before coins, but this ancient chapter of cowrie history cannot be dated precisely. The earliest use of cowrie shells that can indisputably be regarded as money was in north China about 700–200 B.C. These cowries came from south China and Tongking. In the thirteenth century, according to Marco Polo's reports, cowrie shells were still so firmly established in the Yunnan province in southwestern China that taxes had to be levied in cowrie shells.

In India, archaeologists have found cowrie shells associated with coins in sites dating from the first century A.D. From the third or fourth century cowries circulated as

Facing page:

HIGHLAND NEW GUINEA MAN WEARING COWRIE SHELLS

When Europeans first penetrated the highlands of eastern New Guinea in the 1930s, strings of cowrie shells (both Cypraea moneta and C. annulus) were one of the most common media of exchange. This Mount Hagen man wears a typical necklace. In the inland region of Bena a man would work a whole day for six cowrie shells, which Europeans could buy on the coast for about five cents per hundred. Europeans flooded the local economy with so many cowrie shells that they lost their value. In the 1930s the Tsembaga considered cowrie shell ropes essential in marriage exchanges; by 1962 the cowries were worthless. Similarly, the Kakoli included long cowrie shell belts in all marriage exchanges; by the 1960s the Kakoli wore cowrie belts as ornaments without value.

money in the Indian states of Orissa, Udaipur, and Bengal. From Bengal, cowries were shipped over the Himalayas into southwest China. Marco Polo observed this overland trade in the thirteenth century, but undoubtedly the trade long preceded his arrival. In the eighteenth century, cowries were still the only money in circulation in Bengal and they did not disappear entirely until the twentieth century.

The cowrie shells used in Bengal and southwest China came from the Maldive and Laccadive islands off the southern tip of India. These islands supplied the Money Cowrie *(C. moneta)* for most of the world's trade until the eighteenth century. The word *cowrie* is derived directly from the Hindu *kauri*. While traders took shells from the Maldives to China via Bengal, they also shipped them directly to Thailand, where they were currency from the thirteenth to the eighteenth centuries.

Cowrie shells certainly arrived in Africa by the tenth century and probably earlier, preceding European colonization by several hundred years. Ninth- and tenth-century Arab travelers' reports describe cowries traded for African gold; cowries have been found among the cargo of a caravan abandoned in the western Sahara in the eleventh or twelfth century A.D. By the eighth century the Islamic Empire's Spanish sources of gold had been exhausted and the Arabs turned to the ancient West African kingdom of Ghana. Above all else, the Africans wanted cowrie shells in return for their gold. Arab traders shipped the shells from the Maldives, carried them across

HIGHLAND NEW GUINEA MAN WEARING COWRIE SHELLS

the Sahara by caravan and into the sub-Saharan forests of Central and West Africa by river. Long before Europeans arrived, cowrie shells were currency in the cities of Ghana and Timbuktu, in Mali, and throughout central Niger.

Once Europeans established themselves, cowrie shells became the standard currency in West Africa and quickly spread inland. By the middle of the seventeenth century even remote interior regions of the Congo recognized cowries as valuables. European ships brought cowries as ballast on their return trips from India, the Philippines, and Indonesia. At West African ports, the ships unloaded the cowries and traded them for ivory and slaves bound for Europe and the New World. The vast quantities of cowries brought by European ships caused inflation and an enormous decline in their value. By the beginning of the twentieth century, the cost of transporting cowries in most

COWRIE SHELL VALUES

1790	Bambara (Mali; West Africa)	Food for 1 man and 1 horse for 1 day	100 cowries
1890	Mossi (Upper Volta; West Africa)	1 horse 1 basket	70,000 cowries 1,500 cowries
1850	Kuba (Congo; Central Africa)	1 chicken Bridewealth	10 cowries 30 cowries
1907	Kuba (Congo; Central Africa)	1 chicken Bridewealth	300-500 cowries 3,500 cowries

parts of Africa was more than the value of the shells themselves.

Probably because of cowries' success in African trade, European settlers and traders brought Indo-Pacific cowrie shells (both *C. moneta* and *C. annulus)* to North America, where many native peoples readily accepted them in barter. Cowrie shells also circulated as the standard form of wealth in the New Guinea Highlands long before the arrival of Europeans.

TUSK SHELL AND CLAMSHELL MONEY

Other shell currencies include tusk shells, clamshells, and shell bead wampum, all used in North America before the arrival of European settlers.

The Nootka of Vancouver Island, British Columbia, collected Money Tusk, or Dentalia, shells *(Dentalium pretiosum)*, ate the meat of the mollusks, and traded the shells to their southern neighbors. The Nootka were the only fishermen to collect the live Dentalia, which burrow into the mud at twenty-to-thirty-foot depths. They devised complicated dredges for retrieving Dentalia, but even so were lucky to bring up three or four at a time.

The farther the tusk shells traveled away from their source, the more valuable they became. The Yurok of northern California strung their tusk shells on strings twenty-seven and a half inches long. Every Yurok man had a mark tattooed on his arm indicating the exact length a string should be. All the shells on a string had to be the

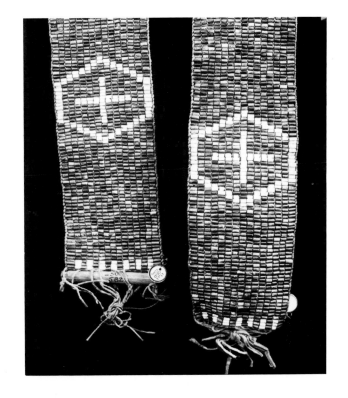

WAMPUM

On the east coast of North America, Indians made rough disc-shaped beads, known as wampum, from the purple and white Quahog or Hard-shell Clam (Mercenaria mercenaria). Precolonial wampum was made of rough discs. Cylindrical beads like these were made after Europeans introduced metal tools. The purple beads made from a narrow band of the shell were always prized over the white ones. Wampum was originally used in ceremonial exchanges, the belts carrying messages of war, peace, negotiations, and alliance. Under colonial influence, wampum gradually became a medium of exchange; by the seventeenth century it was legal currency in both Dutch and English colonies.

SHASTA INDIAN WOMAN WEARING
STRINGS OF DENTALIA SHELLS

same length; larger shells were much more valuable than smaller ones. Shells that made a string of more than fifteen shells were too small to be considered valuable; these were worn as jewelry, but not used in exchanges. An eleven-shell string was so rare and valuable that its owner would be renowned throughout the group.

The nearby Tolowa invariably used ten shells to a string, regardless of length. The longer the string the more valuable it was. A man measured a string by three tattoo marks on his arm. But for both the Tolowa and the Yurok, each tusk shell had the same value as any other one of the same size. Each string of the same length and number of shells was equivalent to any other string, giving this currency exact equivalence, one of the important criteria for money.

The Yurok, and to a lesser extent the Tolowa and Hupa, measured every facet of their lives in precise money values. Tusk shells could purchase a wide range of goods, whose prices were fairly standardized, and virtually all obligations and services from bridewealth to blood debt for murder were valued in tusk shell strings.

The Yurok were preoccupied by acquisition of wealth, in the form of tusk shell strings and also woodpecker scalps and obsidian. They believed that if a man fulfilled all religious obligations meticulously, not only would he have luck in hunting, he would also draw tusk shells to himself. A large collection of tusk shell strings did not automatically confer prestige, but it was a necessary prerequisite: High status in the community could not be achieved without

YUROK DENTALIA SHELL VALUES

A house	3 twelve-shell strings
Small boat	1 thirteen-shell string
Deerskin blanket	1 fifteen-shell string
A bride from a wealthy family	10 strings (various sizes)
Fine for killing an important man	15 or more strings
Fine for adultery	5 strings
Fine for speaking the name of a dead person	2 thirteen-shell strings

such a collection. Other groups in Oregon, Washington, and regions farther north traded Dentalia, but only as one of many valuable materials.

Along the central California coast, the Pomo Indians equaled or even surpassed the Yurok in their preoccupation with accumulating shells. The Pomo were the major suppliers of shell bead valuables to all of central California. Any Pomo could collect Pismo Clam shells *(Tivela stultorum)* and break them into rough small pieces, ready to be made into beads, but only specialists who had inherited the privilege could drill and shape the beads. The driller had to observe certain taboos: He had to work outdoors away from the house and he had to abstain from meat and women; otherwise both his drill and the beads would break.

The Pomo made especially valuable cylindrical beads

CALIFORNIA INDIAN GIRL WEARING SHELL BEADS

This Pomo Indian girl wears her wealth: necklaces of Pismo Clam shell beads. Only women wore such necklaces, but both men and women wore shell and feather belts as a sign of wealth.

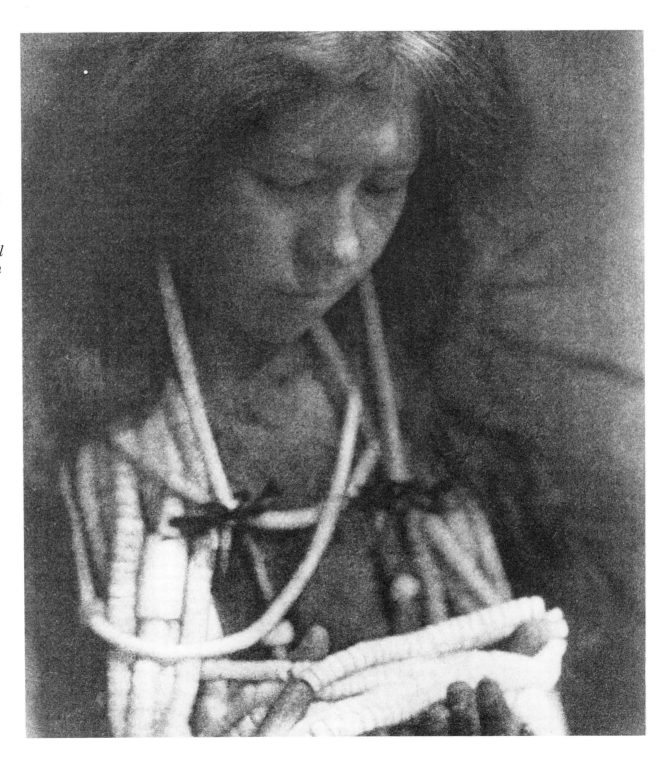

VALUES OF CLAMSHELL BEADS (CIRCA 1900)

A deer	1,200 beads (6 strings)
A domestic bow (8–10 days' work)	2,500 beads (12½ strings)
A good imported bow	4,000 beads (20 strings)

Facing page:

PUEBLO INDIAN MAKING SHELL BEADS

In California and the Southwest the manufacture of highly valued shell beads required a great deal of labor. The artisan first broke the shells into small pieces and then drilled holes by rolling a simple drill shaft with a stone point between his palms. He then strung the pieces and rubbed them on stone to make the beads uniform in size and smooth. In this photograph a Cochiti Pueblo man uses a pump drill, introduced by Europeans, a tool that speeded manufacture and caused the shell beads to become more common and less valuable. Before the pump drill arrived in Cochiti, a three-inch string of shell beads was worth five dollars; by 1897 it was worth only fifty cents.

from the thick heel of the shell. Each was worth from twenty to forty ordinary disc-shaped beads. Beads made of the mineral magnesite were even more valuable than shell beads; each magnesite bead was equivalent to about eight hundred clamshell beads. The Pomo and other central California groups referred to magnesite beads as "gold" and to clamshell beads as "silver."

The Pomo exchanged and offered shell beads on many occasions. They placed them on a corpse as a death offering; relatives gave them to the immediate family of the deceased. A payment of beads to the family of a murdered man satisfied a blood debt in lieu of another killing. Marriages involved a series of exchanges between the families of the bride and the groom. A pregnant woman might be given eight to ten strings of shell beads by her husband's family to "welcome pregnancy"; her own family would give her more beads on the birth of the baby.

Although the accumulation of shell money was a central preoccupation of the lives of both the Yurok and the Pomo, the significance of wealth was quite different for the two peoples. Among the Yurok, money was a means for acquiring power and prestige. Among the Pomo, the accumulation of wealth was an end in itself. As recently as 1940, the Pomo regarded beads and baskets, their symbols of wealth, "as a necessary form of insurance against some dimly sensed, but imminent disaster, which could not be adequately coped with by means of one's inner resources alone." Even though these clamshell bead strings were the standard by which the Pomo measured everything, the shells also had a spiritual dimension unknown to the currencies of modern industrialized nations. After a century of exposure to Western culture and its currency, the Pomo's real wealth was still their traditional valuables, not their dollar equivalents. Whenever traditional shell money has this spiritual dimension, its use is apt to persist even after the adoption of modern currencies.

WHAT IS MONEY?

Despite years of discussions, anthropologists and economists still cannot agree whether such valuables as cowrie shells, the tusk shell strings of the Yurok, or the clamshell beads of the Pomo can be properly called money. The most common definition of money includes four criteria: It must be a medium of exchange, a measure of value, an instrument by which value can be condensed and accumulated, and a standard of deferred payment. It must also be homogeneous, divisible, portable, durable, and all these criteria must exist simultaneously, as they do in American dollars, British pounds, or French francs. From an an-

PUEBLO INDIAN MAKING SHELL BEADS

thropological perspective this definition of "real" money emerges from the particular and complex economic system of modern nations.

In the very different social and economic circumstances of desert hunters and gatherers or tropical forest horticulturists, all the criteria of the economists' definition are rarely found together. In New Guinea the pigs used in exchanges or the enormous stone wheels called "Yap money" are neither homogeneous nor divisible. Pigs are not durable, nor is "Yap money" very portable. In an effort to come up with a cross-cultural definition of money, some economists (known as formalists) define money as anything used as a medium of exchange, while others (called substantivists) distinguish between "general-purpose money," which, like dollars, can purchase all available goods and services and can be used by anyone, and "limited-purpose money," which is restricted to certain exchanges or to particular people.

Here we have limited the word *money* to all-purpose money, to valuables that, like Yurok tusk shells or Pomo clamshell beads, can be used by all members of a society to purchase a wide range of goods and services, and which serve as a standard by which the cost of most goods and services are measured. Exchange systems conforming to these criteria have not developed everywhere in the world. Some important civilizations, like the Maya and Aztec in Mexico and the Inca in Peru, expanded and maintained large empires without the use of anything resembling what economists call money.

In examining shell valuables and media of exchange

from many different societies, we found that most meet some criteria for money, but not all. To understand how each valuable operates within its own economic and social system, we examined each item to determine who could exchange it, for what, and under what circumstances. Those valuables used primarily as gifts or in ceremonial exchanges are especially difficult to fit in to the standard economists' definition of money because what is really being received in exchange are not goods or services but intangibles like power, prestige, friendship, and alliance.

EXCHANGING VALUABLE SHELLS

More varieties of shell valuables are exchanged on the Melanesian islands of the South Pacific than in any other part of the world, but most do not meet all the criteria for all-purpose money. The species of shells that have been valued have differed greatly from region to region and over time. Peoples of New Guinea have used more than ten species of shell as media of exchange—along with feathers, ax blades, and pigs—but shells highly prized in one area or at one time have been almost worthless elsewhere or at different times. Prior to European contact, strings of cowrie shells were the standard media of exchange in parts of the highlands; thirty years later highland people rarely exchanged cowrie shells. Even today Giant Clam shell rings are enormously valuable to some New Guinea peoples, while others never exchange them. The Highland Tsembaga consider Green Turban Snail shells more valuable than pearl shell crescents, while the Chambri of the Sepik

NEW GUINEA "BIG-MAN"

This Mount Hagen man's bamboo breast-plate is a public announcement of his high status; each stick of bamboo signifies a set of pearl shells he has given away.

region judge Green Turban Snail worth only one-twentieth of their most precious valuable—Gold-lip Pearl Oyster shell *(Pinctada maxima)*.

The Chambri (also known as the Tchambuli) cut and ornament Green Turban Snail shells *(Turbo marmoratus)* with coiled basketwork and exchange these cut shells at the many dances and ceremonies of their complex ceremonial life. For the Chambri, no Green Snail shell is exactly equivalent to any other. Each shell, considered either male or female, has its own personal history and a distinctive personality based on markings, size, shape, color, luster, and ornamentation. These attributes distinguish the shells from all-purpose money, which is anonymous: Any two cowrie shells of the same species or any two tusk shells of the same size have the same value. The Chambri use Green Snail shells not only on all ceremonial occasions but also in the marketplace to buy utilitarian items like food, tobacco, or baskets, and as part of the gifts presented to a prospective bride. When the Chambri try to exchange an ornamented Green Snail shell for a net bag, the owner must argue not only about the quality of the bag but also about the value of the shell; no standard exists which pegs one bag as worth a certain number of Green Snail shells.

EXCHANGING SHELLS FOR INTANGIBLES

Although a New Guinea Highlander or a traditional West African might use a valuable shell to buy a sweet potato, a fish, or a canoe, the shell may play a very different role in that society from dollars in modern American society. In preindustrial societies the value of any medium of exchange is apt to be inextricably linked to its social and political significance or to its religious and symbolic importance. To a New Guinea Highlander pearl shell crescents are simultaneously items of wealth that can be accumulated and exchange items to trade for pigs and ceremonial regalia. In Central Africa, the cut cone shell (*Conus* sp.) is a medium of exchange and insignia of high political rank and social status. In exchanges of such shells social and political aims are inseparable from the goal of accumulating wealth.

Many exchanges take the form of competitive gifts: Each round of gift giving creates an obligation to reciprocate. The aim of the exchange is not goods but social status and political power; the person who can give more than he receives increases his prestige and raises his status. One such system is the *moka*, the elaborate ceremonial exchange of the Melpa of the Mount Hagen region of Highland New Guinea. The Melpa try to outdo each other in gifts of pearl shells and pigs. The essence of *moka* is that groups and individuals compete for status by returning in each subsequent exchange ceremony more than they received in the previous one. The Melpa hierarchy of valuables ranks pearl shells highest, followed by pigs. A leader who has gained power through successful manipulation of this exchange system is called a "big-man," and his impor-

CEREMONIAL DISPLAY OF MOUNTED PEARL SHELLS, NEW GUINEA

During an exchange ceremony, people south of Mount Hagen in the New Guinea highlands lay out mounted pearl shell crescents on the ceremonial dance ground.

tance is publicly announced by a large number of bamboo
sticks hanging on his chest. Every man owns a breastplate
of bamboo sticks, each of which indicates a set of five to ten
pearl shells that the wearer has given away. The number of
sticks displays, for all to see, his success—or failure—in
accumulating and giving away pearl shells.

The pearl shells are judged by color and iridescence:
The most desirable have a pronounced reddish or yellow
orange color. When the Melpa present pearl shells in a
moka, they mount them on round resin boards and rub
them with red ocher to enhance their redness. Only
reddish shells are valued as wealth items and given in
ceremonial exchanges and for bridewealth. While white or
greenish pearl shells do not contribute to a man's wealth
and prestige, they are valued as ceremonial ornaments and
may be exchanged in the marketplace. Both ruddy and
white shells are used in direct exchanges for goods such as
pigs or body paint. Worn as ornaments, white pearl shells
are believed to help the wearer gain wealth (reddish pearl
shells) both by making him look impressive to his rivals
and by magically attracting valuables.

In these ceremonial exchanges, Mount Hageners' use
of reddish pearl shell valuables bears little resemblance to
the strict definition of money. No one pearl shell is
precisely equivalent to any other, nor do pearl shells have a
standard value in exchanges for other goods or valuables.
Although reddish pearl shells may be exchanged for pigs,
magic, or the services of ritual experts and may compen-

sate for insults, injuries, or killings, they cannot be exchanged for utilitarian goods such as food or baskets.

For the Tolai of New Britain, another Melanesian island, the route to prestige and power is also through the accumulation of shell valuables. One apparent major difference is that the Tolai simultaneously use Australian currency. When an isolated people comes into close contact with Western society, it frequently discards traditional forms of wealth. But for the Tolai—as for the Pomo of California—the use of shell valuables is so tightly woven into the moral fabric of their society that to abandon them would mean the destruction of their society. The Tolai case is especially interesting in that the two forms of money exist side by side and the people utilize both.

Traditional Tolai money, called *tambu,* consists of yards of tiny nassa shells *(Nassarius* sp.) strung on vines. *Tambu* has not depreciated as sharply as most other Melanesian shell currencies, probably because the Tolai still collect it themselves; Europeans have never bothered to import large quantities of the tiny nassa shells.

Periodically a Tolai will roll up an enormous quantity of *tambu* into a huge coil. These coils are a public display not only of the wealth the owner has already accumulated but also of his confidence in his ability to acquire more, since he cannot use any of the coiled *tambu* for everyday purchases. The coils are displayed at all festivals but may be carved up and distributed only at a man's own funeral or at ceremonies that he sponsors in honor of his clan's recent dead. The route to honor, prestige, and power in

TAMBU VALUES

	1878	1960
1 chicken	¼–½ yard	?
50–60 taro or yams	1 yard	?
1 large canoe	20–50 yards	200 yards

COIL OF *TAMBU* MONEY, NEW BRITAIN, MELANESIA

When this Tolai man completes his coil of tambu, it may contain more than a mile of Nassa shells.

Tolai society lies in sponsorship of many ceremonies, and requires a great deal of *tambu.*

The Tolai have also become successful modern entrepreneurs who use Australian currency to raise and market copra, to buy trucks, and to participate in agricultural cooperatives, but the significance of *tambu* is too deeply embedded in Tolai ceremony and society to be replaced by Australian currency. In Tolai markets, *tambu* can be used interchangeably with Australian currency to buy goods such as taro or fish, but *tambu* can never be bought with Australian currency. *Tambu* remains essential to Tolai society; only *tambu* can be used to pay the specialist who conducts ceremonies, composes dances, and carves canoes; only *tambu* can be given for bridewealth and at funeral ceremonies. As the Tolai say, "For food, money; but for death, *tambu.*" Usually peoples of traditional societies who, like the Tolai, become successful in modern economic terms, scorn traditional forms of wealth and prestige. The Tolai, however, tend to be rich in both *tambu* and Australian cash. They use traditional prestige and power to achieve success in business. In turn, their profits from copra and cocoa plantations, trucks, and copra-buying stations, increase traditional prestige and power.

MAN WEARING ARMBAND OF SHELL
BEADS, SOLOMON ISLANDS

This Malaita man wears an armband
of orange and white shell beads (made
from Jewel Box shells) and black seeds
woven into intricate patterns.

In contrast to the Tolai, the Baegu people of Malaita Island can achieve high status *only* by accumulating shell valuables by traditional means. For them, despite the introduction of Australian money, wealth still consists of strings of orange beads and networks of beads made into belts and armbands. Bridewealth and payments for ritual services must still be paid at least partly in shell valuables. The elders, who still control the wealth, insist that valuables can be acquired only in traditional ways; shell valuables cannot be bought with Australian currency. Even if a Baegu should accumulate Australian currency, he cannot convert such wealth into shell valuables.

Not all ceremonial exchanges involve competitive gift giving. An exchange can establish a friendship, an alliance, or a trade partnership, while further exchanges maintain them. In the Trobriand Islands southeast of New Guinea, one exchange system, usually termed the Kula ring, is a classic example of gift giving that appears voluntary and spontaneous but is actually done out of obligation and self-interest. In this system, Islanders trade Kula bracelets of Leopard Cone shell *(Conus leopardus)* for Kula necklaces of Thorny Oyster shell discs *(Spondylus* sp.). The trade bracelets are exchanged from west to east and the necklaces from east to west, forming a large ring of trading partners connecting many islands. These special bracelets and necklaces can be traded only for each other, never for any ordinary goods. Their exchange establishes and later maintains an alliance between trading partners, who then

KULA BRACELET

This bracelet made of Leopard Cone shell (Conus leopardus) and decorated with seeds and beads is used in Kula ring exchanges in the Bismarck Archipelago near New Guinea.

go on to exchange utilitarian goods like sago, face-paint, and pots. The Kula exchange cannot be understood in purely economic terms: It is a way of establishing and maintaining relationships between individuals and groups.

HOW SHELLS BECOME VALUABLE

How does a particular shell object come to be considered valuable? Economic theory conventionally explains value in terms of scarcity. Where shells are valuable, they have also been scarce, at least in the form in which they are valued. Some shells are scarce 'because they have been transported long distances from their original source, like the Indo-Pacific cowrie shells in West Africa or Thailand. For peoples with only simple tools, deepwater shells like the tusk shells of North America's Pacific coast are scarce because they are so difficult to collect. In Central Africa the cut tops of deepwater cone shells were enormously valuable, until modern deep-sea fishing equipment began to bring up cone shells along with the fish. Subsequently, when the quantity of cone shells available vastly increased, their value declined precipitously until by the 1950s they were rarely used in exchanges anywhere in Central Africa.

The scarcity of shell valuables can also be artificially created; plentiful shells may be valued only in a particular form, like the Giant Clam shell rings of many New Guinea peoples. When only shell beads, rings, discs, or cylinders are valued, common shells are tranformed into a limited resource.

TLINGIT CHIEF WEARING ABALONE-DECORATED CEREMONIAL ROBE, ALASKA

CHIEF'S DAUGHTER
WEARING ABALONE EARRINGS,
BRITISH COLUMBIA

The Indians of the North Pacific Coast prized the blue green iridescence of the southern California Green Abalone shell (Haliotis fulgens) over the pale colors of the locally available abalone shell. The value of the abalone shell depended on the brilliance of its color. The Indians had to instruct the first Spanish traders not to extract the abalone flesh with heat, which alters the color of the shell.

In Oregon and Washington pieces of abalone shell were media of exchange, but for the Northwest Coast Indians, abalone was primarily a precious material for jewelry and decorating precious objects and ceremonial regalia. The size and brilliance of an individual's abalone ornaments attested to personal wealth and status. This chief's daughter wears abalone earrings appropriate to her status. The Tlingit chief wears a ceremonial costume decorated with abalone pieces forming the outline of a brown bear.

Economists' theories about why a particular item should be valued rarely go beyond scarcity. Economic theory cannot help us understand why a scarce shell should be highly valued by one people and not at all by another. The question of why one scarce item is preferable to another led us out of the realm of economics entirely and into the area of cultural values and symbolic significance. As we considered each exchange item, we tried to determine—in addition to who traded it, for what, and under what circumstances—why that particular scarce object was valued rather than another. The answer to this question was often most elusive. Frequently we did not have enough information to hazard a guess.

But where documentation existed, people usually seemed to seize on some physical property of the shell as the essence of its value; for instance, the Melpa of New Guinea valued the redness of pearl shells. Other groups attributed special value to qualities like the luster of pearl shells or the iridescence of abalone shells. On the other hand, value might derive from beliefs about the sea where the shell originated.

In other instances, a shell was valued not for any actual physical property but for a quality that a particular people believed the shell possessed, such as curative or mystical powers. The Australian aborigines traded pearl shells and considered them wealth items, but their value derived from their ritual importance and from beliefs about their mythical origin. In preindustrial society, the value of a shell as an exchange item or as a store of wealth is tightly interwoven with its social and political significance.

WHALE-SHAPED PIPE, WITH ABALONE INLAY, BRITISH COLUMBIA

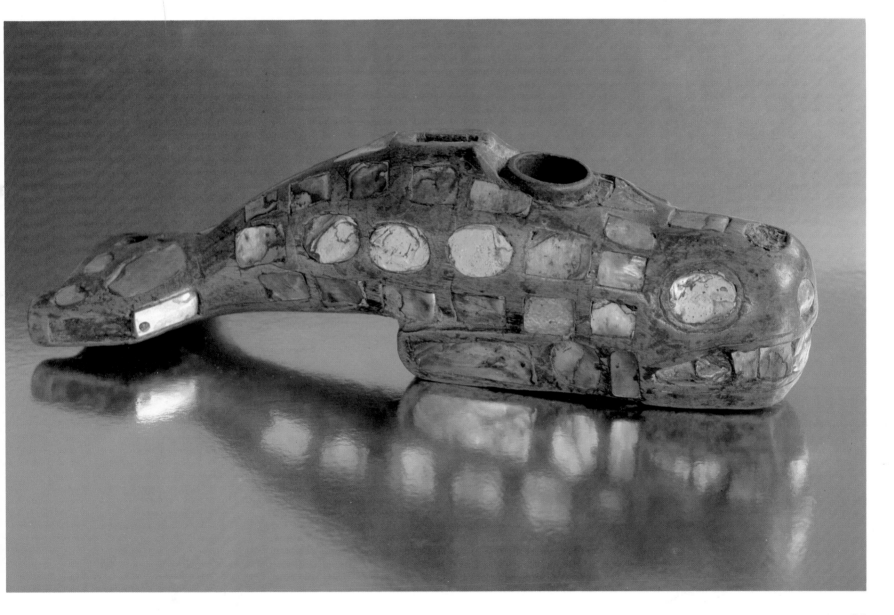

PRE-COLUMBIAN NECKLACE, PERU

WOMAN'S HEIRLOOM, BURMA

This ornament of Sacred Chank shell (Turbinella pyrum), worn hanging at the back of the neck by women of the Chin Hills of Burma, is an example of a valuable restricted in the extreme. These ornaments pass from woman to woman and can be acquired in only two ways: They may be given to the bride's female kin during marriage exchanges or they may be inherited from a female relative. This particular ornament was passed down to a Chin woman from a relative in another region. These ornaments originally came from Haka, where they were used in religious worship, but this significance has been lost; the Chin regard the shells simply as precious heirlooms.

Facing page:

PRE-COLUMBIAN NECKLACE, PERU

This necklace made from pieces of Thorny Oyster shell (Spondylus princeps) was made over a thousand years ago. Thorny Oyster shell was a highly valued material in ancient Ecuador and Peru combining all three conditions of scarcity: It was transported over long distances, its forms required a great deal of labor, and clinging to rocks at depths of twenty to sixty feet, it was difficult to collect. The shell was transported at least a thousand miles from the Gulf of Guayaquil in Ecuador, the southernmost habitat of the Thorny Oyster, to Peru's Nazca Valley, where this necklace was found. Other ornaments made of Thorny Oyster have been found high in the Andes on the Peru/Bolivia border. With the tools available, grinding off the oyster's spiny projections and cutting the shell into uniform pieces must have been a time-consuming process.

DETAIL: DECORATED DENTALIA SHELLS

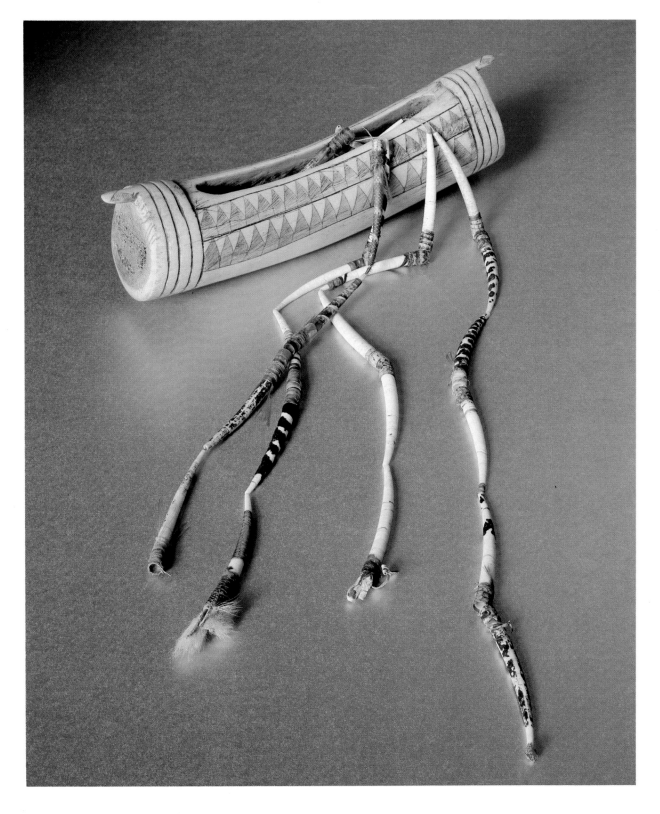

CALIFORNIA SHELL MONEY IN ANTLER PURSE

The Hupa, Shasta, Yurok, and Tolowa Indians of northern California frequently incised dentalia shells with fine geometric designs, wound tiny pieces of snakeskin around them, and attached tufts of red woodpecker down or red thread. The decoration did not increase the shells' value but indicated the value attached to the shell strings. The incised elk's antler purse for keeping dentalia shell strings comes from Oregon. The strings of dentalia shells were collected from the Shasta, Hupa, and Yurok.

SHASTA INDIAN WOMAN WEARING STRINGS OF DENTALIA SHELLS

CALIFORNIA CLAMSHELL MONEY IN TREASURE BASKET

The Pomo Indians of California made some of the finest baskets in North America, decorating them with woodpecker and green mallard duck feathers and strings of beads made from Pismo Clam shells and iridescent Green Abalone (Haliotis fulgens). These treasure baskets, which were in themselves valuable and formed part of marriage exchanges and reckoned as part of a Pomo's total wealth, were used only for storing valuables such as shell beads.

CALIFORNIA INDIAN GIRL WEARING SHELL BEADS

Shells have served as media of exchange all over the world. Top left, clockwise: (1) Disc-shaped pieces of Thorny Oyster shell (Spondylus sp.) from Rossel Island in the Pacific. (2) Strings of orange and white beads cut from Jewel Box shell (Chama sp.) from the Solomon Islands. (3) Tiny Nassa shells (Nassarius sp.) threaded on vine are called tambu by the Tolai of New Britain. (4) A piece of Green Turban Snail shell (Turbo marmoratus), prized by the Tsembaga people of New Guinea. (5) Strings of incised Tusk shells (Dentalium pretiosum) were money for Indians of northern California. (6) A string of alternating black and white shell beads from New Britain, Melanesia. (7) Pieces of Giant African Land Snail (Achatina sp.) from the Congo. (8) Shell rings cut from clamshell and pieces of cone shell (Conus sp.) with intricately cut edges from the Solomon Islands.

VALUABLES FROM THE NEW GUINEA HIGHLANDS

The Tsembaga of highland New Guinea prized pieces of Green Snail shell above all other valuables. The nine Green Snail shell pieces attached to the plaited cord form a waist ornament. The Tsembaga traded feathers and furs to their neighbors in exchange for Green Snail shells, pigs, stone axes, pearl shells, and cowrie shells. They required both shells and stone axes for marriage payments to a wife's kin; the shells were also worn as ornaments on important ceremonial occasions.

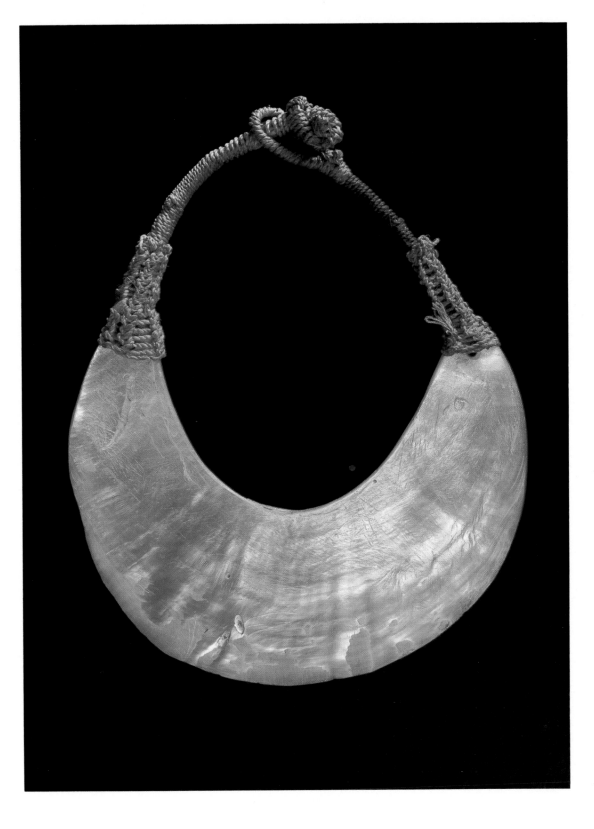

PEARL SHELL NECKLACE, NEW GUINEA

Among the Chambri of New Guinea's Sepik River, this necklace was used only in ceremonial exchanges and for bridewealth payments. It was made from a crescent of Gold-Lipped Pearl Oyster shell, the Chambri's most valuable wealth item, worth twenty Green Turban Snail shells.

NEW GUINEA "BIG-MAN"

DETAIL: SHELL BIB, PERU

BIB OF SHELL BEADS, PRE-COLUMBIAN PERU

Archaeologists often find Spondylus shell in ancient Peruvian tombs with other precious materials, like gold and silver. This bib was part of an extraordinary grave treasure uncovered at Gran Chimu. The multicolored beads made from orange Spondylus shell, purple and white shells, and green malachite form birds and human figures identical to motifs found in ancient textiles. Precisely who wore this bib, on what occasion, and why will probably never be known, but the wearer doubtless was an individual of wealth and importance.

Shells as emblems of status

SELF-DECORATION is universal in human society: There are peoples who wear no clothes, but none who wear no ornaments. The motivation for self-ornamentation may be partly aesthetic, but ornaments, body-painting, and clothing also communicate many kinds of social and political messages. They form a complex of signs that amount to a visual language.

In any simple society, as in a modern industrial nation, ornamentation and clothing immediately identify members of one's own group. Some signs indicate a person's place in society: A married woman may be distinguished from an unmarried one by different dress or an ornament, such as a wedding ring. Those who have undergone initiation ceremonies wear clothing or ornament differentiating them from the uninitiated. Particular kinds of ornament may indicate wealth, high social status, or political authority. A headdress or special emblem may single out the successful hunter or warrior. Some peoples wear elaborate signs of their

Facing page:

DETAIL OF KAP-KAPS, NEW IRELAND

social status at all times; others wear them only occasionally. All peoples have ornaments for special occasions, when individuals display themselves in the greatest possible splendor.

However, not all ornament has social, religious, or ceremonial significance. People may wear jewelry just because they find it attractive—which raises the question of what a people considers attractive or beautiful. This is a complex philosophical and semantic problem as well as a difficult ethnographic one. We have steered clear of canons of beauty and design and concentrated instead on understanding the visual language. We have tried to decipher the message encoded in these exterior signs to discover what they communicate.

Dress and ornament permit members of a group— such as a tribe or language family—to recognize one another. This recognition can be crucial for peoples who live scattered over a large area, enabling them to quickly identify a stranger as either friend or enemy. Similarly, dress and ornament can identify members of a subgroup: Members of the same clan may wear certain clothing patterns; members of a secret society may display an identifying emblem.

Shells are often used as part of the vocabulary of this visual language. We tried to find out not only what information the shell ornamentation communicated but also why these particular shells were chosen—what ideas about the shells made them appropriate in these contexts.

WOMAN'S BELT, EAST AFRICA

When a woman of the Turkana people of Kenya married, she changed her clothing decorated with ostrich egg beads to clothing decorated with cowrie shells. This married woman's belt is made of leather with cowrie shells and beads.

Facing page:

NEW GUINEA GIRL IN INITIATION CAP

During the ceremony of initiation into adulthood, this girl wears a cap of fiber netting decorated with several different kinds of shell. Young Chambri girls of the Sepik River region wore numerous shell ornaments on ceremonial occasions but, after marriage, no longer decorated themselves with shell ornaments.

MARKING RITES OF PASSAGE

Many peoples mark the transitions from one stage of life to the next with ceremonies—rites of passage. Initiation or puberty ceremonies note the transition from childhood to maturity; marriage, another change of status, may mark the beginning of full adulthood. Some societies mark only one or two transitions; in others, each individual must pass through an elaborate series of age-grades or age sets. The person undergoing transition from one social status to another typically wears special clothing and ornament during the liminal phase of the ritual, when he is no longer what he was and not yet what he will be. Once the ceremony is finished and the transition completed, different special clothing or ornament may symbolize the accession to the new status.

The Turkana, Pokot, and Samburu are culturally related nomadic herding peoples of East Africa. All three groups wear elaborate personal ornament both to signal their distinct tribal identities and to display a person's role or rank within the tribe. The wealth of these nomads of the semidesert lands near Lake Rudolf is limited to what can accompany them in their travels: cattle, camels, sheep, goats, and possessions that can be worn or carried. Elaborate hairstyles differentiate initiated men from uninitiated boys. Special ornaments distinguish the warrior. A woman changes her distinctive ornaments at marriage, at first childbirth, at menopause, and at widowhood. Each tribe has distinctive decorations that show a woman's

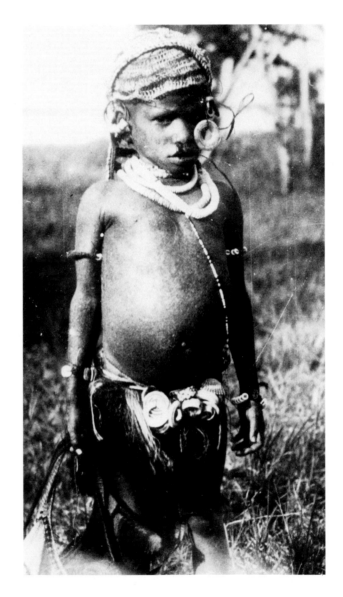

NEW GUINEA GIRL IN INITIATION CAP

marital status: a metal bracelet for married Turkana women, leather bracelets for married Pokot women, and iron armbands for married Samburu women.

Among the Turkana, cowrie shells are one of the markers that distinguish married women from unmarried women. All Turkana women wear leather belts, skirts, and pubic aprons with elaborate decorations. Before marriage, Turkana girls decorate their clothing with ostrich egg beads; at marriage they exchange these for cowrie shells. Among the Galla, cowrie shells designate women's clothing; for the Turkana, cowries distinguish married women from unmarried. (See page 110.)

To these desert peoples the choice of specific material or form appears to be arbitrary. There does not seem to be any particular reason why ostrich eggs should be associated with unmarried women and cowrie shells with married women. The important point is that the materials must differ not only from one another but also from those used by neighboring peoples.

In all parts of the world the married state is signaled by some special form of ornamentation, sometimes worn by both husband and wife, often only by the wife. In New Guinea among the Mountain Arapesh a Green Tusk shell *(Dentalium elefantinum)* is the insignia of a woman's married status. During the wedding ceremony a Green Tusk shell with a red feather is inserted into a hole which has been specially made in the tip of a woman's nose. Judging from photographs of the Arapesh, the bride wears the shell only during the ceremony, although the hole remains permanent.

KALASH WOMEN OF AFGHANISTAN

These cowrie-covered headdresses communicate the group affiliation, the gender, and the marital status of their wearers. Kalash women of the Pakistan/Afghanistan border begin wearing this distinctive woolen headdress decorated with stripes of Ring Cowrie shells, bells, and buttons when they are promised in marriage at about age four. From that time the Kalash girl or woman is expected to wear her six- to seven-pound headdress at all waking moments, even at home or while working in the fields. Ethnography from other groups of this region often mentions cowries as insignia of status. In the Waigal Valley of Afghanistan both men and women wear cowrie shell rosettes as symbols of high rank; renowned warriors are distinguished by bandoliers decorated with cowrie shell rosettes. These peoples probably do not associate cowrie shells with any specific status, but rather consider them simply as an appropriate material for emblems of general social status.

In parts of north India, especially Bengal, a Hindu woman's equivalent of a wedding ring is a bracelet made of sections of Indian (or Sacred) Chank shell *(Turbinella pyrum)*, usually lacquered yellow and red. These bangles are believed to contribute to the husband's prosperity and longevity; hence, his wife never removes them as long as he is alive. If he dies, the widow removes the bracelets, breaks them, and throws them away.

Although we could find no statement about why chank shell was used for wedding bracelets, other ritual uses of chank shell yielded clues. In both south and north India some castes blow chank shell trumpets during wedding ceremonies, accompanied with recitations such as: "May Ganges water and sea-chank betide enduring bliss to bridegroom and bride." In the wedding ceremonial, the chank shell, blown as a trumpet or worn as a bracelet, appears to be an auspicious symbol promoting lasting good fortune for the married couple.

Across the border from northern India, in the Himalayan countries of Nepal, Sikkim, Bhutan, and Tibet, neighboring peoples practice a similar tradition with a different meaning. Women of this mountainous region between China and India frequently wear chank shell bracelets but not as emblems of marriage. As in India, once the bracelet is put on, it is not removed. The bracelet, wide but of relatively small diameter, is placed on a girl's wrist when she is very young; by the time she is grown, she can no longer remove it. Unlike in India, this practice

SACRED CHANK SHELL BRACELET

This bride from north India wears a wedding bracelet made from Sacred Chank shell.

appears to be restricted to women of low social and economic status. The religion of the region is a mix of Hinduism and Buddhism. Since Buddhists, like Hindus, consider the chank shell an important auspicious symbol, the bracelet could be meant to bring the wearer good fortune.

Special clothing or ornament is usually worn during a ritual of transition; other special ornament is put on at the completion of the ceremony to denote the wearer's new status. The people of the Andaman Islands in the Indian Ocean do things a little differently. Their shell ornaments do not change; rather, the acts of taking them off and putting them back on signal the beginning and end of their rites of passage. Most Andaman celebrations or ceremonials are characterized by people dancing; painting themselves with red ocher and white clay; and wearing necklaces, dance skirts, armbands, and leg bands of netting and shells, principally tusk shells *(Dentalium* sp.) and cockle shells *(Cardium* sp.). However, before any rite of passage, including initiation ceremonies, weddings, and funerary rituals, the participants are stripped of all ornament. When the transition is completed, they paint themselves and put back on their cockle and tusk shell ornaments; they have arrived at the next life stage.

At a funeral, not only the dead but also the mourners go through a rite of passage. Relatives of the deceased remove all ornaments from the body before it is buried.

ANDAMAN ISLAND MEN

Andaman Island men greet each other. They both wear girdles, leg bands, necklaces, and armbands of dentalia and cockle shells.

During the mourning period, mourners must abstain from their usual red and white body paint and wear special mourning clay. They cannot wear shell ornaments or participate in dances until the deceased has completed the final life passage, the journey to the world of the dead. While the soul of the deceased is en route to the land of the dead, the deceased and the mourners are both in a liminal state, symbolized by the removal of shell ornaments.

When the journey is complete, two ceremonies take place. During the first ceremony, which ends mourning, relatives put on their shell ornaments and their usual body paint, and dance. During the second ceremony, the bones of the deceased are exhumed and, like the relatives, painted with red ocher and white clay and decorated with cockle and tusk shells. Relatives of the dead person then wear these bones as amulets to prevent or cure illness.

The Andaman Islanders apply similar decorations to inanimate objects. When an Andamaner finishes making a basket, he decorates it by hanging shells from the rim; a completed canoe is painted red and white and adorned with shells. When these decorations fade or deteriorate, they are not refurbished. The addition of shells and paint appears to signify the completion of another sort of transition: the transformation from living plant to basket, from tree to canoe—from a natural state to a cultural artifact.

ANDAMAN ISLAND GIRL WEARING SKULL AMULET

This young girl wears her sister's skull as a protective amulet. The skull has been encased in netting, painted with red ocher and hung with dentalia and cockle shells.

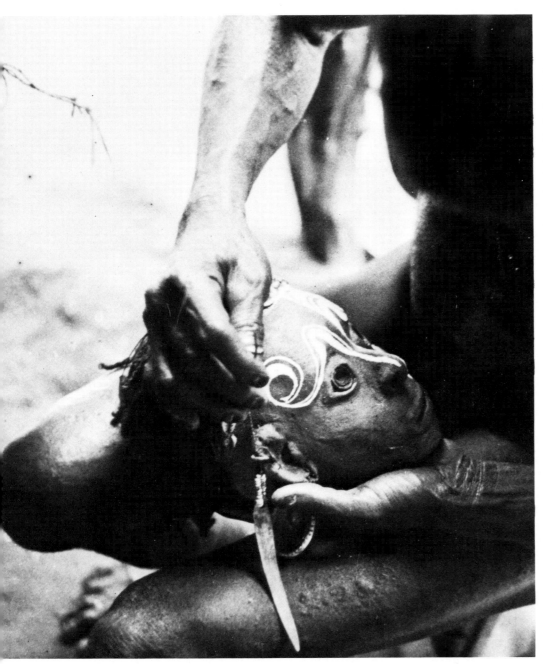

IATMUL ARTISAN PAINTING A SKULL

When a Chambri or Iatmul from New Guinea's Sepik River region dies or when an enemy head is taken in battle, the head is kept until all the flesh has disappeared from the bone. A craftsman then covers the skull with a mixture of oil and clay, modeling the features. He paints the face with patterns matching the face-painting that person used in life. The band placed above the forehead signifies something about the person's status during life; for example, a band of opossum fur signifies an initiated man. The row of Ring Cowrie shells (Cypraea annulus) on this skull means that the man was important and wealthy. Although the Chambri—unlike the peoples of the highlands— have never been known to use cowrie shells as exchange items, they did consider all shells valuables.

DECORATED SKULL,
NEW GUINEA

SHELLS AS INDICATORS OF SOCIAL AND POLITICAL RANK

Some societies restrict particular ornaments to certain people, signifying their membership in an exclusive group, or their high social or political rank, or their singular military achievements. As signs of particular status, these ornaments are comparable to a fraternity pin, an old school tie, or a royal crown. Unless observers understand the messages that these symbols communicate, they might easily mistake them for purely arbitrary decoration.

In Africa, cowrie shells, primarily media of exchange in many regions, are symbols of royal authority and power for the Kuba of Zaire. The king and members of royal lineage are called *Baapash,* "people of the cowrie shells." This name may refer to the wealth in cowries that the king receives as annual tribute or, on a more general level, to cowries as an emblem of royalty. The persons who may wear cowrie shells are strictly prescribed; only descendants of royalty may wear any kind of cowrie borders on their clothing. The number and position of cowries adorning a Kuba signals political rank. All men of royal descent, wives and sisters of chiefs, and their children may wear cowrie-decorated armbands, but only the highest nobility may wear leg bands or headdresses decorated with cowrie shells.

Cowrie shells figure prominently in ceremonies and myths surrounding Kuba royal succession. The king is the focus of Kuba belief: Regarded as a god on earth, he is the

A KUBA CHIEF

This Kuba chief holds high rank within his society, as can be seen from the numerous cowrie shells he is entitled to wear.

source of all authority, power, and fertility. A king's death is an extraordinary event in Kuba life. His death is kept secret for the first three days; then funerary ceremonies begin. On the sixth day the dead king is dressed in cowrie-covered robes and a cowrie-studded mask (the *mwaash a m'booy)* and buried with valuables—including cowrie shells—and a royal slave who is buried alive with him. His successor undergoes nine days of coronation ceremonies, during which he receives instructions and the symbols of kingship. These rituals, which emphasize the continuity of the dynastic line, are followed by a ceremony in which the new king's sons and grandsons present him with an offering of cowrie shells, signifying their loyalty. The new king's direct descendants promise to put down any revolts against him or his lineage. The ceremony also acknowledges and pays homage to the powers of fertility residing in the king.

After spending three months in seclusion, while a new capital is constructed, the king begins his reign. The act that finally makes him king, proving his right to succession, is the act of sitting on the royal stool, which is a basket covered with cowrie shells. The Kuba firmly believe that if anyone not destined to become king sat on this cowrie-encrusted stool, he or she would be struck dead instantly. Like the shells offered by the sons and grandsons, the shells on the stool appear to refer to succession and the continuity of the royal lineage.

The last part of the succession ceremonies consists of nine days of initiation rites for boys. During the initiation ritual the cowrie-studded mask *(mwaash a m'booy)* is usually displayed on a hilltop. The mask, which signifies the king's power, represents Woot, the mythical first ancestor of all Kuba, the creator of the Kuba people, the origin of all fertility. Woot was also the first Kuba king from whom all subsequent kings are believed to have descended. As first king, he decreed the Kuba social order: matrilineal succession, the political structure, initiation. During the ceremony, the king wears the mask and plays the role of Woot. Only the king, Woot's direct descendant and the embodiment of his attributes, is permitted to wear this mask. Besides cowrie shells, the mask includes many other royal symbols, including the leopard skin on the face and the representation of an elephant's trunk and tusks. The only clue to the ideas underlying this use of cowrie is that since Woot is believed to have come from the sea, the cowries may have been associated with his marine origin.

In most societies where individuals can accumulate wealth, riches and high status go hand in hand. When a person wears or displays the objects that constitute his wealth, the distinction between wealth item and insignia of status can be difficult to make. One useful criterion is whether or not the people who accumulate ornamental wealth items are permitted to wear them. One African example is the cone shell discs that circulated widely as media of exchange in Angola, Zambia, Mozambique, and southern Zaire. Cut from Leopard Cone *(Conus leopardus),* Betuline Cone *(C. betulinus),* and Prometheus Cone *(C. prometheus),* they were commonly called *mpande* shells. In the mid-nineteenth century the British explorer and mis-

KUBA MASK, ZAIRE

sionary, Dr. David Livingstone, reported that two cone shell discs could purchase a slave, while five bought an elephant's ivory tusk. Anyone might own a cone shell disc, but in most tribes only individuals of high rank could wear them as ornaments, although the precise category of high-ranking personage varies from group to group.

Among the Ba-ila people of Zambia, only chiefs wore the cone shell discs; the higher a chief's rank, the more shells he was privileged to wear. Among the Vahumbe of Angola, wives and daughters of chiefs could wear leather pendants ornamented with cone shells. Unlike the shell discs, these ornaments were not media of exchange. They could be neither bought nor sold; a woman obtained them by inheritance or gift. Anyone could trade these shell discs for cattle or ivory, yet they were emblems of status that only a few had the right to wear—a not uncommon paradox.

In traditional societies of the Pacific islands from Hawaii to New Guinea, where rank and hierarchy are major principles of social organization, the material most commonly used as insignia of high rank is shell. Throughout Polynesia and Melanesia, certain shell ornaments are worn only by the island elite.

These shell insignia of high rank were also valuables. Most of these valuables, however, could not be freely converted into other valuables or goods and services. They could be exchanged in restricted contexts, if at all. Many could be acquired only by gift or inheritance. Hence, one way a person of high rank could maintain and extend his social and political power was to lend valuable insignia to an ally or kinsman on special occasions.

HIGH-STATUS VAHUMBE WOMAN, ANGOLA

Wives and daughters of Vahumbe chiefs are entitled to wear this leather ornament decorated with Prometheus cone shell discs and brass.

The traditional society of the Melanesian islands of Fiji was consumed with concern about rank. While some Pacific island groups were quite egalitarian, with rank dependent on personal effort, Fijian rank was elaborate and strictly hereditary. Every clan and subclan, and each family within a subclan, had a definite position on the socioeconomic ladder. Within a family, each member was ranked according to age. Each village had a rank; each chief was ranked according to the position of his village and clan. The high chief was not only at the political and social pinnacle but was also considered sacred. Touching a high chief or anything he had worn was a crime punishable by the loss of a finger or even death.

One of the most famous emblems of Fiji's high chief was the Golden Cowrie shell *(Cypraea aurantium)*. In 1853 a British naval officer, John Erskine, whose ship stopped briefly at Fiji, noted that on great occasions important chiefs each wore two beautiful orange cowrie shells. He also commented that chiefs sometimes "lent them [the shells] to a friend to enable him to make a figure at a ceremonious feast." Although later writers offer little specific information about the wearing of the Golden Cowrie, we do know that throughout these islands wearing rare and valuable objects was the exclusive prerogative of high-ranking personages.

Besides the Golden Cowrie, shells appear in several other contexts on Fiji. The Fijians' most valuable material was whale's tooth ivory imported from the neighboring Tonga Islands. Fijians combined whale's tooth ivory with Black-lipped Pearl Oyster shell *(Pinctada margaritifera)* in a

ZAMBIAN CHIEF WEARING CONE SHELL DISCS

Chief Shaloba of the Ba-ila people of Zambia in southern Africa wore numerous cone shell discs showing that he was very important.

KAP-KAPS, NEW IRELAND

WAR LEADER, SOLOMON ISLANDS

Throughout the Solomon Islands and Bismarck Archipelago the wearing of kap-kaps—clamshell discs overlaid with tortoiseshell filigree—appears to be restricted to men of high status. This war leader of the Baegu people of Malaita Island in the Solomons wears ceremonial regalia. Among the Baegu the kap-kaps pass from father to son.

breastplate that remained a prerogative of nobility well into the twentieth century. Different sources describe these breastplates as worn by senior chiefs, or by older nobles, or by warriors in the most noble dance. Use of the breastplates probably varied somewhat over time but always remained reserved for those of highest rank. Another item restricted to chiefs was a kind of cowrie shell of unspecified species attached to chiefs' houses and canoes. The most likely candidate is the Egg Cowrie *(Ovula ovum)*, which only nobles on the island of Manus in the Admiralties may wear, attach to their houses or to their canoes.

In many Melanesian societies, especially in New Guinea, New Ireland, New Britain, and the Solomon Islands, intense competition among individuals for high status contrasts with the fixed hereditary hierarchy of Fiji. A "big-man," as a Melanesian leader is called in pidgin English, the lingua franca of the region, is self-made, although sons of wealthy and powerful fathers have a definite advantage. A "big-man" acquires wealth, prestige, power, and the allegiance of many allies and followers through clever manipulation of economic exchanges, which in most groups include shell valuables. He advances himself not by hoarding wealth but by giving away or lending it, so that those who receive his valuables are in his debt. Someone who also demonstrates mastery of magic, gardening, and oratory, as well as bravery in war, will become an especially prestigious and powerful "big-man."

Among the most striking insignia of "big-man" status are discs of Giant Clam shell *(Tridacna gigas)* overlaid with

BREASTPLATE, FIJI

Breastplates of whale's tooth ivory mounted on Black-lipped Pearl Oyster shell were worn by men of high status on the Melanesian island of Fiji.

tortoiseshell filigree. These *kap-kaps*—the general name, although each group may have its own term—are worn on the head in the Solomon Islands and on the chest in New Britain and New Ireland. Information about *kap-kaps* is scarce. We do know that on New Ireland only "big-men" are permitted to wear *kap-kaps;* young men and women never wear them. In the Solomons a man may inherit a *kap-kap* bequeathed along family lines, although not necessarily from father to son, but he must earn the right to wear it. There appears to be no connection between the *kap-kap,* or its particular filigree design, and clan membership. (See color plate, page 84.)

Special Status: The Warrior

Throughout Taiwan, the Philippines, and the highlands of Southeast Asia, shell ornaments almost always signify a special kind of high status: the warrior or war leader. In the mountains of south Asia, Taiwan, and the Philippines, we were struck by the frequency with which shell ornaments and shell-decorated clothing were worn by warriors who brought home many enemy heads. From Assam and Burma to Formosa and the Philippines, much of men's ceremonial clothing and self-decoration signifies martial achievements. Observers have long noted both tattooing and red clothing as common warriors' insignia throughout the region. But they had not noted how often shells appear as part of this symbolic complex. The practice is so ancient that the original symbolic meaning is probably lost.

One early written reference can be found in Sung

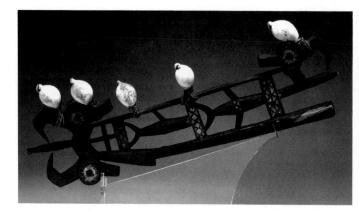

CANOE PROW, ADMIRALTY ISLANDS

NOBLE'S HOME, ADMIRALTY ISLANDS

WAR DANCER, ADMIRALTY ISLANDS

On the island of Manus in the Admiralty Islands near New Guinea, society was divided into two classes: the nobles, called Lapan, and the commoners. The use of Egg Cowrie shells (Ovula ovum) was restricted to members of the noble class. Only Lapan could hang Egg Cowries on their belts, their canoes, and their houses. Wearing a bandolier of Egg Cowries and dogs' teeth was a privilege accorded only certain of the highest-ranking families. The Egg Cowries on this wooden canoe prow indicate that a noble family owned the canoe. The carved fish on the prow probably have a symbolic or protective significance.

Egg Cowries are also associated with warriors. War leaders were always chosen from noble families. A warrior, like the one in this photograph, wears a large Egg Cowrie on his penis both when he performs a war dance and when he goes into battle. The practice of permitting a warrior, who is a commoner, to wear insignia otherwise restricted to the noble class appears to be prevalent in Melanesia and island Asia.

Dynasty documents (A.D. 960–1279), which describe mountain tribesmen in Yunnan province in southwest China near the Burma border going into battle with armor and helmets covered with cowrie shells.

In modern times, in Assam, not far from Yunnan, in the Himalayas on India's Burma border, the Nagas were still using cowrie shells as warriors' insignia. One of several Naga subgroups, the Angami Nagas, describe all male ornaments as signifying exploits in war. Three rows of cowrie shells on a man's kilt meant that he was a successful warrior; a fourth row was awarded only to warriors of great renown. Only a man who had killed in battle could wear a breast ornament of cowrie shells, wood, and red-dyed goat hair suspended from a cloth band decorated with cowrie shells and hair from a slain enemy. A famous warrior might wear as many as three breast ornaments at a time. Bands decorated with cowrie shells and worn on a man's arm indicated that he had brought home an enemy arm; a band on the wrist meant an enemy hand; on the ankle, an enemy foot. Angami Naga women never wore cowrie shell ornaments; these were a quintessentially male symbol, a sign of military achievement.

Although most of the Naga tribes share similar symbolic elements associated with warriors—feathers, red-dyed animal hair and fibers, buffalo horn, and monkey skulls, as well as cowrie shells—these appear in different combinations with somewhat different meanings. Among two subgroups, the Rengma and Sema Naga, women were allowed to wear cowrie shells, signifying their husbands'

NAGA WARRIOR

This Angami Naga is apparently a highly successful warrior, judging by the many rows of cowrie shells on his kilt, though the nineteenth-century European traveler who drew his portrait may have assumed the cowries were simply decorative and exaggerated their number.

heroic deeds. For yet another Naga group, the fourth line of shells signified not martial achievement but successful love affairs.

South of Assam, the Haka Chin of Burma are another mountain people whose warriors ornament themselves with cowrie shells. A Haka Chin went to war primarily for booty, taking heads not to increase his prestige or well-being in life but to add to his store of merit in the afterworld. A war leader's gunpowder horn shows many of the same decorative elements associated with warriors from Assam to the Philippines. The horn made from wild bison is decorated with designs in red and black lacquer and silver inlay and hangs from a strap of red cloth decorated with cowries (see page 117). This strap reminds us of the Naga breastplates hung on straps decorated with cowrie shells. It also resembles bandoliers decorated with nearly identical rosettes of cowrie shells worn by distinguished warriors in the Waigal Valley of Afghanistan. Such similarity in both form and significance is unlikely to be purely coincidental, but we could not uncover the precise connections.

On the island of Taiwan, shells were associated with both political leadership and with warriors. Taiwan has a considerable population of indigenous peoples culturally related to those of the Philippines and highland Southeast Asia. Rugged mountains have effectively isolated the estimated forty thousand original inhabitants from the Chinese immigrants in the western part of the island. Although all the groups speak related languages and most

LAKHER MAN WEARING GUNPOWDER HORN, HIGHLAND BURMA

are subsistence farmers, their social and political organization displays great diversity: from the rigidly stratified
classes of the bilateral Paiwan and Puyana of the south
coast, to the informally organized, dispersed settlements of
the patrilineal Bunun in the central highlands, to the
Atayal in the north who live in compact villages with
nonhereditary leaders chosen from village ritual groups.

Despite their differences, certain themes have been
common to almost all of these groups, the most striking of
which is the importance of headhunting. Among the
Paiwan, whose sociopolitical system is rigidly hereditary,
successful headhunters were rewarded with privileges
otherwise restricted to nobles. For the groups whose
leadership was not determined exclusively by birth, the
route to leadership lay in military prowess and success in
bringing home heads. The indigenous peoples of Taiwan
share this emphasis on headhunting with many peoples of
highland Southeast Asia and the Philippines.

The Paiwan people of Taiwan's south coast have a
highly stratified society composed of three classes: high
chiefs, secondary nobles, and commoners. An elaborate
visual vocabulary of clothing and ornament expresses a
Paiwan's precise rank. Only nobles may wear black, dark
blue, or purple clothing, fabric with embroidered or woven
designs, and certain styles of trousers and skirts. Among
ornaments restricted to nobles, one of the most striking is a
hat decoration made of a cone shell disc (*Conus* sp.) and
boar's teeth. Both men and women wear these ornaments;
a high-ranking chief might wear several at once. A

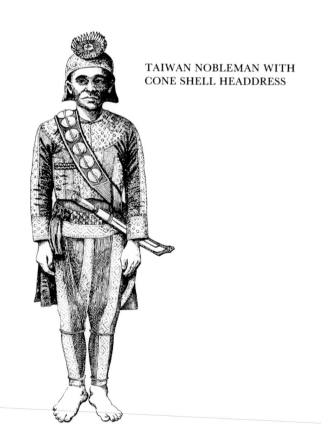

TAIWAN NOBLEMAN WITH
CONE SHELL HEADDRESS

BAGOBO WARRIORS WITH SHIELDS, PHILIPPINES

commoner who has distinguished himself in battle may be granted permission to wear the rosette.

For both the Bunun of the central highlands and the Atayal of the north, pieces of cone shell served as public tally of the number of heads a warrior had taken. Only headhunters could wear cone shell discs. The number of discs on a man's clothing signified the number of heads he had taken. The Bunun also wore headbands made of rectangular pieces of shell when they went into battle; each shell plaque represented a head that a warrior had taken.

In the Philippine Islands, head-taking was also very important. The Kalinga and Igorot of northern Luzon took heads primarily for prestige, although the Igorot also claimed that the practice ensured the success of their harvests. Among the Kalinga and the Igorot a man was not considered fully adult nor was he permitted to marry until he had taken at least one head in battle. As in Taiwan and many places in the highlands of south Asia, the successful head-taker was entitled to special insignia: for the Igorot and Kalinga, a tattoo and a decorated shell. For the Kalinga, and probably also the Igorot, a large Black-lipped Pearl Oyster shell *(Pinctada margaritifera)* incised with geometric designs signified that its wearer was an adult male who had taken at least one head in battle. The incised pearl shell was a man's most valuable possession—so valuable that many men entitled to wear it were not able to acquire one.

IGOROT MAN, PHILIPPINES

An incised pearl shell worn at the waist signified that its owner had taken a head in battle and was therefore a marriageable adult.

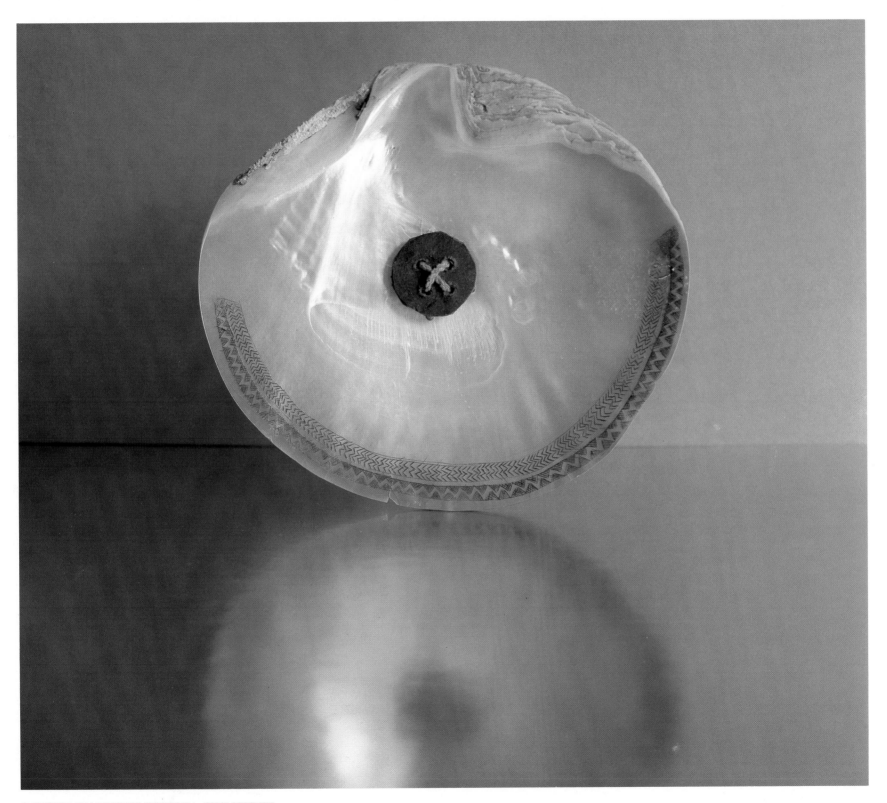

KALINGA WARRIOR'S INSIGNIA, PHILIPPINES

GALLA DANCE BELT, ETHIOPIA

Facing page:

GALLA DANCE BELT, ETHIOPIA

The Galla wear different ornaments according to age, rank, wealth, and the occasion. This dance belt is decorated with Ring Cowrie shells and pendant Dove shells. In Galla ritual language, the cowrie is synonymous with woman and vagina and is usually worn only by women. When boys weave cowrie shells into their braids, the shells signify their immaturity. The Galla also put cowrie shells around the necks of babies to protect them.

To those who understood, this belt undoubtedly communicated something about the wearer's rank and the occasion when she would wear it.

DETAIL: DANCE BELT, ETHIOPIA

KUBA MASK, ZAIRE

N'TOMO MASK, WEST AFRICA

Among the Bambara people of Mali, each male is initiated into his first age set at adolescence; thereafter, he enters a new age set about every three years. Each age set owns certain masks and dances that form a major part of all Bambara festivals.

The N'tomo society is a secret society in which young boys are taught Bambara ideas about the nature of mankind and the universe. Unlike most Bambara masks, which portray animals, the N'tomo masks are horned human faces studded with cowrie shells; they represent humanity in its original state of beauty and innocence. The Bambara believe that the first human could not speak; thus the masks have no mouths. The number of horns ranges from two to eight, with each number representing some aspect of humanity; the increasing number symbolizes the initiate's growing knowledge. The eight-horned mask represents the highest level of understanding, when human beings recognize their own mortality. The cowrie shells on the N'tomo masks represent both the human skeleton and the multitude of mankind.

Facing page:

KUBA MASK, ZAIRE

The mwaash a m'booy mask represents Woot, the first king and ancestor of all the Kuba. It can be worn only by Kuba kings.

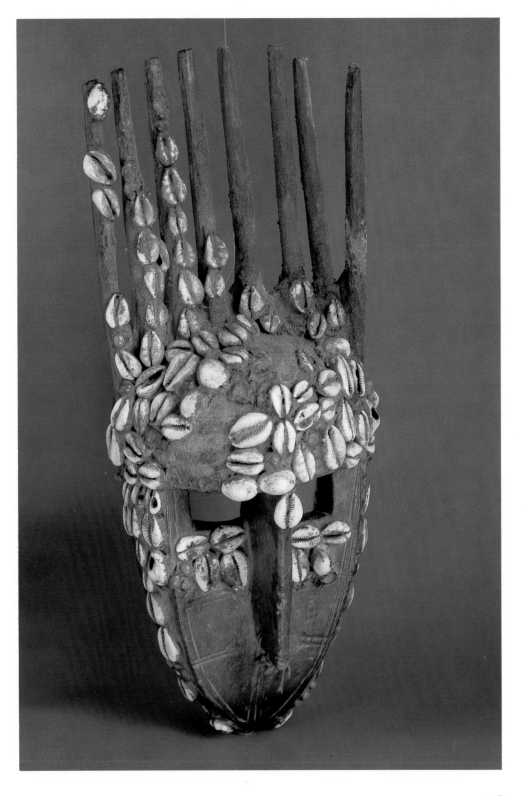

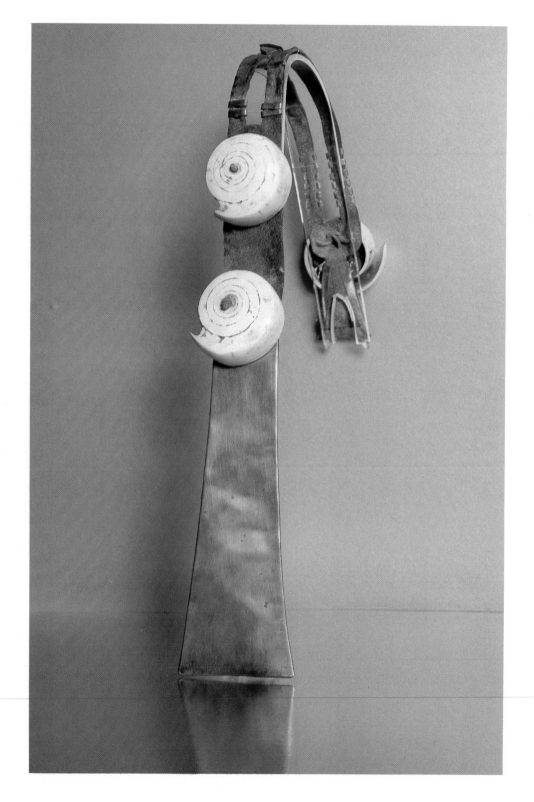

HIGH-STATUS VAHUMBE
WOMAN, ANGOLA

NOBLEWOMAN'S
ORNAMENT, ANGOLA

WARRIOR'S ORNAMENT, NEW GUINEA

A New Guinea warrior usually wears this ornament—made of Egg Cowrie shells (Ovula ovum), Nassa shells (Nassarius sp.), and fiber—hanging around his neck, but when he goes into battle, he holds it in his teeth to look as fierce as possible. The man below wears a similar object.

NEW GUINEA WARRIOR

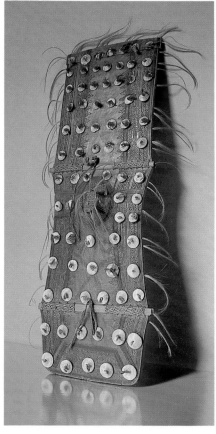

PHILIPPINE WAR SHIELD

On the Philippine island of Mind-anao the Bagobo used this wooden war shield, displaying elements common to shields in other parts of the Philippines and Southeast Asia: cone shell discs, red cloth, and red-dyed hemp fiber. However, the choice of cone shell is unusual for the Bagobo; cowrie shells on their war shields were a more common decoration.

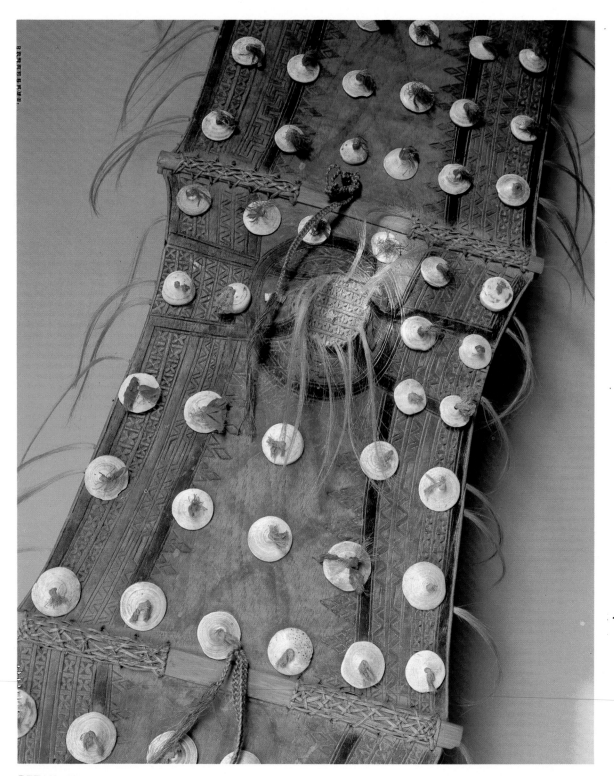

DETAIL: PHILIPPINE WAR SHIELD

GUNPOWDER HORN, BURMA

This gunpowder horn was made by a Chin chief while he was in jail following a Chin uprising in 1918. Since all chiefs were subsequently given rifles, the chief never had occasion to use it. Made from bison horn, it is decorated with red and black lacquer and silver inlay and suspended from a cloth strap decorated with cowrie shells. The collector of this gunpowder horn considered it the finest piece of Chin artistry he had ever seen. The man carrying a very similar powder horn is a Lakher, neighbor to the Chin in the mountains of highland Burma.

LAKHER MAN WEARING
GUNPOWDER HORN, HIGHLAND
BURMA

CHIEF'S HEADDRESS ORNAMENT, TAIWAN

This headdress ornament of cone shell, boar's teeth, and glass beads was worn by nobles and distinguished warriors of the Paiwan people of Taiwan. The ornament below is attached to a hat decorated with beads and cowrie shells. In the drawing, the chief's ornament is attached to a leather helmet, worn by a nobleman who also wears a bandolier of what appears to be cone shell discs. For the Bunun and Atayal, shell discs signify the number of heads a warrior has taken in battle; they may have served the same purpose for the Paiwan.

TAIWAN NOBLEMAN
WITH CONE SHELL
HEADDRESS

LIME SPATULA, NEW GUINEA

Some artifacts from New Guinea also reveal an association of shells with head-hunting. This bird—probably a hornbill—formed the top of a spatula that the Mundugumor of the Sepik River dipped into a container of lime when chewing betel nut. Each pendant string of Nassa shells and feathers signifies a head its owner has taken. In a similar manner the Kaup people of the Sepik put strings of Nassa shells around the tops of their ceremonial spears, each circle of shell representing one head taken.

Shells in ritual and myth

AMONG the most intriguing shell artifacts are those linked to magic, ritual, and myth. Even more than dress or ornaments, ritual objects are expressions of an elaborate visual language, giving concrete form to the intangible. They may refer to a fairly simple concept or embody a whole complex of social or political ideas. They may express a people's ethical values and their cosmological beliefs, operating simultaneously at several levels of meaning.

Shells are often used by sorcerers and curers to work their magic. Some people believe shells have inherent power; others believe that a sorcerer or curer must activate latent power in shells or that he must introduce power into them. The sorcerer uses a shell's power to influence natural forces, such as the weather, or to cure the sick, to protect someone from evil, or to harm an enemy.

The forest-dwelling peoples of central and southern Africa believe sorcerers have the ability both to cure and

Facing page:

DETAIL: KUBA MASK, ZAIRE

121

to cause illness and death. For these sorcerers the Giant African Land Snail *(Achatina* sp.) has particularly potent powers.

The Lunda of Barotseland in Zambia regard the Giant Land Snail as a dangerous weapon. Lunda sorcerers have animal familiars (evil spirits) under their control. The familiar is not just an evil companion but also the sorcerer's agent, capable of seeking out victims and even murdering them, depending on the sorcerer's instructions. When a snail shell has been properly prepared by the sorcerer, filled with mud—and probably other hidden substances—from which several short sticks emerge, it is a particularly dangerous familiar. According to Lunda belief, this snail shell familiar goes out at night carrying a knife, crawls into victims' houses, and cuts their throats. Any severe attack of pain in the throat may be attributed to a snail shell familiar.

We found a snail shell apparently identical with the Lunda's Giant Land Snail shell in the American Museum of Natural History, but it belonged to the Lulua or Bakete people of the Kasai, not far to the northeast of Lunda in Zaire. The Lulua, unlike the Lunda, believe that such fetishes are not always evil; their power can be used also in a beneficent way. Lulua sorcerers use snail shells both to contain magical medicine and to enhance the power of other fetishes or amulets like the wooden fetish figure with snail shell and animal horn containers hanging on its back. This carved figure has no power of its own; a sorcerer must endow it with power through reciting incantations, attach-

CONGO FETISH FIGURE

ing natural objects such as the snail shell and animal horn, and putting magical substances into the shell and horn containers. The Lulua also believed that the presence of a snail shell hung by a person's bed increases the power of the sleeper's other protective amulets. Sorcerers of the nearby Luba, on the other hand, use snail shells alone, hiding them near the dwellings of those they wish to harm.

Intrigued by this widespread use of Giant Land Snail shells in South and Central African sorcery, we tried to discover peoples' ideas about this creature that might underlie its use in sorcery. Detailed ethnographies told us that sorcerers carefully chose horns to use as containers for magical substances according to the symbolic associations with the particular animal from which each horn came, suggesting that similar symbolic associations must also underlie particular uses of land snail shells. Our only hint in written sources was a spiral symbol that the Lulua use as a tattoo, incise on objects, and paint on walls, and which they liken to a snail shell. The spiral sign, with regular stripes dividing it into equal sections, signifies the passage of a person's life moving alternately through good and evil, but how this idea about snail shells might relate to the sorcerer's use of shell remains unclear.

For Australia, where shells are part of sorcery and curing over much of the continent, we had greater success in understanding the ideas underlying sorcerers' ritual objects. Australia's deserts are among the world's environments least hospitable to human life. Extremely low rainfall makes agriculture impossible; small nomadic bands of aborigines subsist by hunting game and gathering scarce food plants. The aborigines' meager material resources and simple technology contrast vividly with the richness and complexity of their religious and social life. Small bands gather together in considerable numbers for the many ceremonies that make up the annual cycle of rituals. Aborigine myths not only explain the origins of every animal, plant, rock, pool, or other feature of the landscape but also relate human beings to every natural part of their environment. Rain, crucial to survival in the desert, is a major focus of ritual and belief.

Objects made of Black-lipped Pearl Oyster shell (*Pinctada margaritifera*), originally from the Broome area on Australia's northwest coast, frequently appear in sorcery, curing rituals, and in rainmaking ceremonies. Pearl shell is one of a number of materials rare in the desert—like quartz, tektites, and even plastic—which the aborigines believe were left behind by mythological beings of the Dreamtime, a kind of timeless mythic past. The peoples of Australia's interior had no knowledge of the shells' actual marine origin; they did not even know large bodies of water existed. These pearl shells were also valuables that could be exchanged for other goods, passed along trade networks stretching across the continent. Designs incised on the pearl shells were rain symbols, like snakes or rain clouds, but since only the carver usually knew the meaning of particular designs, the message in the pattern was often lost by the time incised shells reached interior deserts.

PUBIC PENDANT FROM AUSTRALIA

The Pitjantjara people wore this pearl shell pendant in rituals to attract rain.

The aborigines believe that all materials left behind by the Dreamtime Beings have potent powers that a trained sorcerer may use for either beneficial or harmful purposes. The Pitjantjara people of the Gibson Desert use both pointers and curing discs of pearl shell. Their sorcerers use pointers to project illness or death into an enemy or to drive away harmful spirits. These pointing instruments may also be made of bone, wood, or stone, but those made of pearl shell are especially powerful. As the sorcerer points toward the victim, he sings an incantation. The power of the weapon flies through the air and enters the victim through one of the body openings.

The Pitjantjara use discs of pearl shell principally for curing. One name for a native curer *(Ma:banba)* defines him as the possessor of the shell disc *(Ma:ban)*. The initiation of a curer includes "shooting shell discs into various parts of his body." The discs in his ears give him power to hear and understand everything; those in his jaw permit him to speak to spirits. Discs in his stomach render him invulnerable to injury; in his forehead, they grant the power to divine and to see into a patient's body to diagnose illness. When the curer uses this X-ray vision to diagnose the patient, he presses his curing disc to the patient's body. The disc is believed to pass right through the body, removing the disease-causing substance.

Pearl shells in aboriginal ritual and ceremony are always associated with rain and rain beings. Not only is rain essential to human survival in the desert, but the Rainbow Serpent, the creator of rain, is the source of all

MAN WEARING PEARL SHELL PENDANT, NORTHWEST AUSTRALIA

magical potency, fertility, and of all human life. Different groups use pearl shells in various ways in rainmaking rituals. In the Gibson Desert a sorcerer scrapes the edges of a pearl shell and mixes the powder with fresh grass or human semen. In the Kimberleys region, pearl shells are broken and placed in a waterhole. The Jigalog of the Western Desert say that pearl shells attract rain because the Dreamtime Beings who are responsible for rain wore pearl shell decoration while they wandered about in the Dreamtime. The Jigalog place bits of pearl shell in bands on the upper arm and forehead or swing around a long spear fitted with small pieces at its end to attract rainmaking spirits. During rainmaking ceremonials, they wear large incised pearl shells as pubic ornaments both as a means of attracting rain and as insignia of ritual rank.

In most ritual contexts the pearl shell is also associated with the life-giving powers of rain and the Rainbow Serpent. For curers pearl shells are a powerful healing agent; during female initiation ceremonies in the Great Victoria Desert, the initiate is considered dead until the power of the pearl shell symbolically brings her to life.

In Australia pearl shell was the sole species used in ritual; peoples of another desert, the Pueblo Indians of the American Southwest, use many species of shells in their elaborate rituals.

The name *Pueblo* refers to a number of closely related groups of whom the Zuni and the Hopi are the largest and best known. Today the Pueblo Indians depend primarily on agriculture for subsistence, although in the past they supplemented their diet with game. While the village is the basic social unit, social organization varies from one to the next. All Pueblos, however, share the same religious beliefs, with variations in specific myths and rituals. Village rituals are mainly concerned with controlling the forces of nature: change of seasons, coming of rain, growth of crops, curing of illness. Each village also has many religious societies, each with its own rituals for specific functions: One group controls rain; another, game animals; a third, witches; a fourth, war.

Shells used in Pueblo rituals include abalone, olivella, bivalves, and gastropods. Unlike the aborigines of Australia's interior, who were ignorant of the existence of the ocean, the Pueblo Indians knew that the shells that they received in trade from tribes farther west originated in the sea. On rare occasions they even made the long and difficult journey to the Pacific to collect shells themselves.

One of the most powerful Zuni fetishes was the "Big Shell," a large white (unidentified) univalve shell that priests of Zuni's Big Shell Society blew as a trumpet and from which the priests derived their power.

In one Zuni myth, the Zuni are forewarned of an enemy attack. First the priests of the Big Shell Society blow the shell into a bowl of medicine water, poisoning the surrounding springs; any enemy or his horse who drinks from the springs swells up and dies. As the enemy force approaches the Zuni, the priests blow the Big Shell. All the enemy soldiers tremble, bleed, and fall dead. In another

NAVAHO MAN WEARING
FETISH NECKLACE (see page 158)

myth, the Big Shell kills by emitting thick noxious black fumes with an overpowering smell. The Zuni, however, no longer have their powerful Big Shell. According to their traditions, toward the end of the last century the Big Shell priests and some witches began to feud. When the Big Shell people used their shell to kill one of the witches, other Zuni became afraid that the priests might begin to use the shell against innocent people as well as Zuni enemies. The Big Shell was buried and never found (to the regret of some Zuni who during World War I wanted to use it against the Germans).

Another shell that the Pueblos associate with war is the olivella or Dwarf Olive shell *(Olivella biplicata)*. This tiny white shell, called the "heart shell of war," is the emblem of the soldier. Priests of the war society wore bandoliers of olivella shells combined with the scalps of enemy victims. The Zuni decorate miniature bows and war shields with olivella shells; these tiny replicas are attached to prayer sticks placed on the altar of the war gods' shrine. These gods grant victory in battle but also have power over success in all human affairs, and influence forces of nature that control rain and success of crops.

Rain is as crucial to the Pueblo Indians as it is to the Australian aborigines. A major part of the Pueblos' elaborate ceremonial life is devoted to ensuring the rain necessary to the success of their principal crop, corn. The only explicit reference to the meaning of shells in Pueblo myth and ritual describes shell as belonging to a category of sacred hard substances that also includes turquoise and

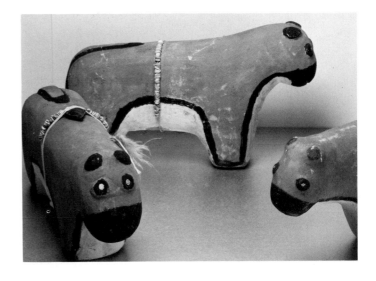

ZUNI HUNTERS' FETISHES

The Zuni believed that these mountain lion images were actually petrified mountain lions. Members of the hunters' fraternity made offerings to the mountain lions to ensure success during hunts for animals that are their prey. To begin such a hunt without the fetishes' help was considered futile. However, the fetish figure was impotent until a Zuni priest consecrated it with a string of shell beads and an arrowpoint. The beads bring the mountain lion to life and give it power. Even when not attached to the hunting fetish, shell attracts game. The Zuni sprinkle shell mixed with cornmeal under the body of a slain deer to ensure success in killing more deer; the Hopi put a shell bead into a coyote or fox trap to "invite the animal in."

coral. However, careful examination of all the contexts in which shells appear suggests further symbolic associations.

During virtually all Pueblo ceremonies sacred water representing the sacred springs, the home of the spirits responsible for rain, stands on the altar in a container that is either a pottery bowl or a large marine shell: either ark shell *(Arca* sp.), *Glycemeris,* or abalone *(Haliotis* sp.), or large bivalve. During ceremonies a Pueblo priest frequently sprinkles sacred water from the shell or offers it in a smaller shell for participants to drink. The link between shells and sacred water is consistent with Pueblo belief in both the sacredness of the ocean where the shells originated and in a mythical unity of all sacred water: ocean, rain, and sacred springs. Of course, sacred water in the form of rain is necessary to grow the corn on which the Indians depend. According to myth, the corn maidens, the spirits of the corn, fled to live with the spirits in the sacred springs because the Indians were careless with their corn. In an annual corn ceremony the Zuni entice the corn maidens to return and to bring with them sacred water so that when they plant corn the rains will come.

Pueblo rituals frequently combine shell with corn as well as with water. An offering of corn pollen in an abalone or bivalve shell is frequently placed on an altar, as is prayer meal, a mixture of cornmeal and shell fragments considered food for the spirits. In Pueblo ritual surrounding childbirth and naming, either the mother or child is touched with shells or with sacred water administered

KACHINA DANCERS (see page 159)

from shells. These ceremonies suggest a parallel between sacred water in the form of rain, promoting healthy growth of corn, and sacred water associated with shells, fostering the growth of the child.

While iridescent Green Abalone shells *(Haliotis fulgens)* usually appear only in the context of sacred water and rain, white shells have more complex symbolic associations. One important deity for most Pueblo groups is a female spirit called White Shell Woman or Hard Substance Woman. According to the Zuni the shell fragments used in prayer meal are rubbings from her body. The sun lives in White Shell Woman's house, from which he rises in the morning and to which he returns at night. All Pueblo groups associate the color white with the east—the only color that all groups consistently associate with the same direction—thus linking white shells with the rising sun, as well as with sacred water and corn.

In choosing shells as symbols, the Pueblo peoples focus primarily on some natural quality: Their marine origin links shells with sacred water; their hardness associates them with Hard Substance Woman; the whiteness of certain shells connects them with the east and the rising sun. On the other hand, the link between olivella shells and the war gods seems to arise from some quality imputed by Pueblo myth and thought, rather than from any natural shell characteristic.

To the Yoruba of West Africa, shells are also one element

PLAINS INDIAN CHIEF

of an elaborate symbolic language expressed in ritual, art, and myth. Nigeria's fifteen million Yoruba, united by common language, history, myth, and ritual, are divided into fifty kingdoms, each ruled by its own *oba,* or king, and subordinate chiefs. Traditionally, Yoruba men have been farmers and skilled craftsmen, especially in metal, while Yoruba women are famous traders. The Yoruba have been known even in precolonial times for their huge markets and for their cities.

The Yoruba have hundreds of deities, each associated with certain natural materials, costumes, artifacts, and dances. Anthropologists who have studied the Yoruba have given detailed explanations of almost all ritual symbols. The Yoruba carefully choose each element of each ritual object for its symbolic associations with a particular deity or ritual. Our research turned up many ritual objects decorated with cowrie shells, but a search of anthropological literature uncovered only the assumption that cowrie shells were money. In view of the detailed symbolism attached to all the other materials connected with ritual objects, this explanation seemed inadequate.

Hunting for the meaning of Yoruba ritual cowries, we began by looking for every published reference to shells in Yoruba myth, ritual, or proverb and by looking at all Yoruba objects ornamented with cowrie shells, hoping to discern threads of common meaning. We quickly noticed that cowrie shells were always associated with some deities and never with others. When we consulted an expert on

Facing page:

PLAINS INDIAN CHIEF

The clamshell disc that this nineteenth-century Sioux chief wears at his neck represents the sun. Plains Indians believed in a force that pervaded the universe but was especially evident in the sun. This power might manifest itself in a dream in which a person or animal offered to confer certain powers, if the dreamer followed specific instructions. A Blackfoot medicine man recounted a dream in which an old man appeared offering him a shell necklace that, when worn, would give him power over the weather. During the Sun Dance, this medicine man used his shell necklace to prevent rain. The Omaha believed the sun to be such an important source of power and protection that they appealed to it for protection only for the most important occasions, like a long journey or a battle. The Sioux chief in this photograph probably wore the clamshell disc to invoke the sun's power for his personal protection and to ensure military victory.

YORUBA PRIESTESS,
NIGERIA

*This Yoruba priestess
wears strings of cowrie
shells.*

cowries, he pointed out a further distinction. Although all cowrie shells on the Yoruba artifacts look similar, two distinct species were represented: Money Cowrie *(Cypraea moneta)* from the Indo-Pacific Ocean and Ring Cowrie *(C. annulus)* from the east coast of Africa. These two species turned out to have a very different history. Many centuries before European traders came to Africa, highly valued Money Cowries were imported from India and carried by caravan across the deserts and down the Niger River into West Africa. Only in the nineteenth century did Europeans introduce Ring Cowries, which the Yoruba accepted as money but never considered as valuable as the original Indo-Pacific Money Cowries.

Closer study of the Yoruba artifacts revealed a difference in the ritual contexts in which the two species of cowries appeared. Ring Cowries decorate artifacts connected with divination and the god Eshu. Cowries are often used in divination; the diviner must be paid for this service. Eshu is best known as the trickster, but he is also god of the marketplace—where cowries traditionally were used as money—and acts as messenger or intermediary between human beings and the gods. Like the diviner, Eshu must also be paid for his services. These contexts are consistent with cowrie shells' narrow meaning as money, leading us to speculate that Yoruba associations with these recently introduced shells are essentially limited to money.

In contrast, Money Cowrie shells (despite their common name) do not appear to be associated primarily with money. Money Cowries appear on artifacts associated with all the White Gods, especially Obatala, chief of the White Gods and creator of life, and with Orisha Oko, god of agriculture and the fertility of the earth. Money Cowries also appear on objects associated with Shango, god of thunder and with Shopona, the smallpox deity. No species of cowrie shell appears in any association with Ogun, god of metal and war, or Odudwa, god of the earth and ancestor of the Yoruba kings.

Obatala and all the White Gods are responsible for the creation of human beings and the fertility of women. Orisha Oko is responsible for the success of crops and the fertility of the land. Shango, god of thunder, was originally all red, but Yoruba myth explains that when he married Obatala's daughter, he took on some characteristics of his father-in-law, becoming half red and half white. We hypothesized that cowries are associated with those gods that the Yoruba characterize as white, life-giving, creative, curing, tranquil, and cool, as opposed to those deities (e.g., Odudwa and Ogun) characterized as red or black, hard, hot, and responsible for war, metal, political systems, and destructive forces.

Studies of iconography of Nigerian art supported this hypothesis, suggesting that coolness is an important and desirable virtue in West African thought and art, signifying calm, balance, harmony, social stability, healing, rebirth, and purity. Its opposite, heat, is considered highly dangerous. Symbolically, coolness is linked with whiteness; the Yoruba White Gods are also cool. The Yoruba associate such white materials as cowrie shells, chalk, white feathers, and ivory with these gods. Among the Igbo, Nigerian neighbors of the Yoruba, images of coolness also include luster that does not tarnish; cowrie shells, unlike most shells, are naturally lustrous and never need polishing.

For the Bini, another group related to the Yoruba, whiteness symbolizes ritual purity, good fortune, and fertility; all natural objects used in rituals for the chief of the Bini White Gods are not only white but also must be smooth, cool, and found near water. Yoruba logic also links water with purity, and, in ritual, water is a cooling element. The cowrie shell appears to epitomize this category of natural objects: It is white, naturally and permanently lustrous, smooth, cool, and connected with the properties of water: purity and coolness.

Having clarified the link between cowrie shells and the White Gods, we still had to deal with the apparent anomaly of Shopona, the smallpox deity. Eventually the rituals and myths associated with Shopona revealed that the link between the cowrie and this god had nothing to do with whiteness, coolness, water, or the White Gods: The significant aspect of the cowrie that linked it to Shopona was its shape. The Yoruba regard smallpox as a manifestation of the earth; in fact, Shopona is often called Lord of the Earth. The earth nourishes the Yoruba, giving them millet, corn, and other grains, but the earth also sends punishment in the form of smallpox. The Yoruba believe that in the course of this disease "the grains men have eaten come out on their skins." Shopona images are frequently covered with cowries representing these grains, the pustules of the disease. Cowrie shells associated with Shopona objects are frequently dyed with blue indigo, considered a royal and auspicious color. The dye may have been applied because the whiteness would be symbolically inappropriate in this context.

Another shell frequently offered on the White Gods' altars is that of the Giant African Land Snail. This rough, dull brown object bears little resemblance to the cowrie shell; its symbolic significance is linked to characteristics of the living creature inside rather than the appearance of the shell. The Giant Land Snail secretes a clear or whitish fluid, which the Yoruba perceive as white, cooling, and bloodless—in opposition to hot, dangerous, red blood. Like water, the snail's secretions are used in ritual to "cool" the gods when they are too "hot." While both snail shells and cowrie shells are presented as offerings, cowrie shells primarily adorn images, altars, and worshipers—as symbols epitomizing whiteness and coolness. The snail, on the other hand, plays an active role in rituals by counteracting the dangerous heat of the red and black gods.

SHELLS AS SYMBOLS

For the Yoruba, the whiteness and luster of the cowrie shells are significant in symbolically connecting them with the White Gods, while their shape makes them appropriate decoration for the smallpox goddess. The land snail's role in Yoruba ritual is based on the biological characteristics of the creature inside the shell. For the Pueblo Indians of the American Southwest, the watery origin of the shells is crucial to their association with water and sacred rain. In Australia, ritual pearl shells' significance grew out of their origin in the mythical Dreamtime, a quality that existed solely in the minds of the aborigines. Each people seizes on characteristics of the shell or mollusk, which they associated with some symbolic, ritual, or mythical element of their own society.

The quality of a shell most frequently seized on as symbolically relevant is color. Whiteness can have a wide range of symbolic associations: east and the sun among the Pueblos; purity, coolness, fertility among the Yoruba; mother's milk and semen among other African groups. The meaning of a white shell becomes linked to whatever meaning whiteness holds for a certain group.

The Andaman Islanders of the Indian Ocean metaphorically equate the iridescence of pearl shells with lightning. They say that lightning is the flash of a pearl shell thrown across the sky by the goddess Biliku. She also uses the shell's sharp edge as a knife to cut off the head or limbs of a wrongdoer.

On the other side of the world, in California, the Pomo Indians construct a similar metaphor. They associate lightning with the iridescent gleam of the abalone shell (*Haliotis* sp.), and believe that Thunder Man, the deity responsible for both lightning and thunder, has eyes of abalone shells and wears a coat covered with them. Lightning flashes when he blinks his eyes; thunder rolls when he shakes his coat.

HIGHLAND NEW GUINEA MAN IN CEREMONIAL DRESS

In highland New Guinea the Melpa of the Mount Hagen valley equate whiteness with brightness. They believe that all bright decorations attract both valuables and the opposite sex. This man dressed for a ceremonial has painted his face black to enhance the brightness of the pearl shells, báler shells, and cone shells with which he has decorated himself.

An analogy between the shape of a shell and some other natural phenomenon is often the basis of its symbolic importance. In South America the Saha of the Colombian Andes make shell offerings to the spirits. For an offering to ensure the goodwill of the spirit of the snow-covered mountain, they choose a limpet shell *(Fisurella nimbosa)*, which looks remarkably like a mountain, green in the lower parts and white around its peak. If a Saha diviner determines that a child's severe illness is caused by the spirit of a dead ancestor who wants the child as a helper in the afterworld, the family makes an offering to substitute for the living child. This offering, which represents the child, takes the form of shells resembling male or female sexual organs: a turret shell *(Turritella gonostoma)* for a boy or a *Cyphoma gibbosa* for a girl.

Because many peoples perceive a resemblance between cowrie shells (usually *Cypraea annulus* and *C. moneta)* and the human eye, cowries have frequently served as protective amulets against the evil eye. Believers in the evil eye hold that someone may willfully or unintentionally cause harm by looking at another person or animal with envy or admiration. Children and domestic animals are thought to be especially vulnerable to these glances. Belief in the evil eye exists in peasant societies throughout Europe, North Africa, the Middle East, India, Latin America, and the Philippines, but it is strongest around the Mediterranean, in the Middle East, and northwest India.

The idea of the evil eye dates back to the ancient Egyptians; both beliefs and symbols associated with it have remained remarkably consistent throughout two thousand years over many thousands of miles. The same amulets against the evil eye reappear in different eras and places: a clasped hand, blue beads, red tassels, mirrors, and cowrie shells. Cowries and facsimiles made of clay and precious metals are common finds in ancient Egyptian tombs. Strabo, a Greek historian of the first century B.C., mentioned women in Upper Egypt (the Sudan) wearing shells around their necks as protection against what is translated as "fascination." In Latin, the phrase for evil eye was *oculus fascinus.* Whether the Sudanese women were actually wearing their shells as amulets against the evil eye may be open to question, but Strabo's interpretation shows that the idea of shells as an effective shield against the evil eye was perfectly understandable to ancient Greeks.

Even today, in Italy, Spain, and Egypt, children, in particular, frequently wear cowrie shells to ward off dangerous glances. In northwest India, cowrie shell amulets are especially evident on valuable oxen and cows, while in Arab countries, both people and domestic animals often wear protective cowries.

Some peoples attach significance to a particular mollusk's behavior. One example is the land snail's ability to withdraw into its shell. In South America, the Desana of Colombia's tropical forests believe that malevolent spirits cause illness. During curing ceremonies they invoke the

BAGOBO GIRL WEARING SHELL BRACELET

The Bagobo people of the Philippines believe that any closed circle forms a protective barrier that evil influences cannot penetrate. Because these bracelets cut from Leopard Cone shells (Conus leopardus) form a closed circle, they are believed to protect the wearer from harm.

land snail so that the patient may be hidden from the evil spirits that caused his illness, as the soft vulnerable body of the snail is hidden inside its shell.

Both the behavior and the habitat of land snails have symbolic importance for another South American people, the Kaatans of Bolivia. The Kaatans attribute magical properties to natural objects that combine different elements—like the snail, which can live both on land and in the water. .

The Ifugao of Luzon Island, the Philippines, make an association between the operculum of a shell and deities who control birth. A most distinctive ornament that Ifugao men wear on special occasions like dances or funeral processions is a belt of discs made from opercula of the Green Turban Snail *(Turbo marmoratus)*. From this belt hangs a wooden scabbard in which a man keeps his bolo knife, which he uses for both hunting and war. These belts are heirlooms of considerable value; one generation hands down the pieces of opercula to the next. Since they are no longer made, these belts have become rare. A century ago probably five men in thirty owned such a belt; today fewer than one in thirty may possess one.

These belts always have a large central disc with carved edges, the *upud*. Although the belt is worn only by men and carries a weapon used in hunting and war, its central disc represents a curious obstetric deity, Pumupud, who is or becomes a *upud*. This unpleasant deity causes difficult births by blocking the birth canal and obstructing the infant's passage. The Ifugao greatly desire children

IFUGAO MAN IN CEREMONIAL DRESS, PHILIPPINES

This Ifugao man from the Philippines wears a belt made of the opercula of Green Turban Snails. The central disc represents a deity who causes difficult birth.

and regard such a hindrance as evil.

If the Ifugao, an inland people, are aware of the origin of the disc from which they make this ornament, there could be a logical association between the operculum and the deity. The operculum is the mollusk's trapdoor, which closes the opening of the shell, preventing any predator from attacking the soft and vulnerable body within and thus paralleling Pumupud's obstruction of the birth canal. However, we could not find out whether the Ifugao themselves make such an analogy. A further relationship between men, hunting, and reproductive deities is expressed in the Ifugao belief that the gods of reproduction and fertility carry all living men in a blanket sling, as Ifugao mothers carry their babies. In hunting ritual men pray to the gods of reproduction to hold them tightly, protect them, and render their hunt successful. This relationship between the gods of reproduction and the gods that obstruct birth and why the latter should be the centerpiece of a man's scabbard belt remain unclear.

SOUND IN RITUAL

Another important quality of shells frequently used in rituals is their capacity, as trumpets and rattles, for making sound. Such instruments are part of rituals throughout the world; the sound usually is a means of communicating with the supernatural. Rattles can summon, repel, or control spirits; trumpets carry a prayer to the ears of a deity, signal spirits or participants in a ceremony.

The Jivaro Indians of South America use the sound of shell rattles to control the vengeful souls of slain enemies. The Jivaro, who live in the tropical forests of Ecuador, are fierce headhunters. The trophy heads that they bring home from expeditions present a great danger: If an enemy's soul escapes from its head, it will avenge itself by killing the slayer or one of the slayer's relatives. The purpose of the famous Jivaro custom of shrinking heads is to prevent the enemy's soul from escaping. During the festival that takes place after successful raiders return to their own village, Jivaro women wearing dance belts made of pieces of land snail shell suspended from fabric perform dances in which they hop up and down, making the loudest possible sound with their snail shells. Along with the sound of drums and flutes, the percussive sound of these snail shell rattles appears to be essential to prevent enemy souls from escaping from the trophy heads. At the end of the feast the enemy souls are expelled and sent back to their homes, where they will no longer threaten Jivaro warriors and their kin.

Although another South American forest people, the Desana of Colombia, believed land snails had protective powers, nothing in the available ethnography suggests that the Jivaro chose the snail shells for reasons other than their availability and noisemaking potential.

Rattles are an essential part of shamans' curing rituals among Indians of the North Pacific Coast of North America. Northwest Coast Indians believed that all illness was of supernatural origin: Either the soul had wandered

JIVARO WOMAN WEARING DANCE BELT

ALASKAN TLINGIT SHAMAN CURING WITH A WOODEN RATTLE

from a person's body, or else witchcraft had driven a disease-causing object into the patient. Shamans had the gift of curing—and causing—such illnesses. To perform a cure, the shaman needed a spirit helper, whom he summoned with dancing, singing, and the percussive sound of a rattle. The most familiar Northwest Coast rattles are made of wood, beautifully carved in the form of animals. The Gulf Salish of British Columbia and the Tlingit of southern Alaska frequently used rattles made of scallop shells *(Pecten caurinus)*. While, in principle, all members of the society, including women and children, used rattles in ceremonies, scallop shell rattles appear to have been restricted to shamans.

In the Philippines a shell tinkler sounds a warning to evil spirits. The Iloko people of Luzon Island make wind chimes by hanging discs of Capiz or Window Pane Shell *(Placuna placenta)* from a ring of fiber. They suspend the shell tinklers under the eaves of a house, in front of the windows, where the sound of the shells striking against one another will keep away harmful influences.

Shells are just one among many objects—sticks, bones, claws, stones—that can produce percussive sounds. For these ritual shell rattles, their significance lay in the sound they produced. The shells themselves did not appear to have symbolic meaning. The choice of shell over other materials seems to have been based on their availability and the quality of their sound.

The number of natural objects that can produce sounds when blown is much more limited than the

YUROK GIRL WEARING DANCE SKIRT

Women of Oregon's Hupa and Yurok peoples wore ceremonial costumes decorated with pendant Pink Abalone, clam, and snail shells. In Yurok and Hupa ceremonies, the jangle of the suspended shells warned the other participants of the arrival of the priestesses. Even an accidental glance at the priestesses would result in bad fortune. Since the shells were of considerable worth, these ceremonial skirts were also valuable heirlooms.

materials suitable for rattles. Reeds and bamboo can be made into flutes, animal horns into trumpets, but probably the most common ritual trumpets are shells. While rattles are apt to play a minor role in ritual or belief, shell trumpets frequently possess great spiritual power. They have been central symbols in the religions of India, China, Tibet, and ancient Mexico.

Shell trumpets are especially evident on the Pacific Islands. In Fiji, warriors blew Triton's Trumpets *(Charonia tritonis)* before going into battle and as part of a chief's funeral rites. In the Solomons, Eddystone Islanders blew shell trumpets to signal their return from successful headhunting expeditions.

In India, Tibet, and China the chank shell is a focal symbol that embodies many aspects of belief. The chank in India appears in Hindu ritual and iconography: Its use as a trumpet, its white color, its spiral shape, and its marine origin are all symbolically significant. In Hinduism, whiteness signifies purity and absence of pollution, a central concern of this religion. Another Hindu symbol of purity is the sea; everything that emerges from the sea is considered pure.

Ritual use of the chank as a trumpet is mentioned in very early sacred texts and still occurs in ritual as a call to prayer and as an essential part of many marriage ceremonies and other rituals. In some regions of India the chank serves as a container for sacred water during worship; a worshiper pours sacred water from the shell over the image of the deity on the altar. The power of the

FIJIAN BLOWING
TRITON'S TRUMPET

sacred chank is so great that ordinary water poured into it is transformed into sacred water.

The chank shell most frequently appears in Hindu iconography as a symbol of Vishnu, one of the two most important gods of the Hindu pantheon. Vishnu is always portrayed holding a chank shell; a chank shell can replace his statue or picture on an altar. Several elements symbolically link Vishnu and the chank: Both have their origin in the sea, most of Vishnu's symbols are spiral in form, and the sound of the chank trumpet may be associated with Vishnu as the creator of speech.

In Tibetan Lamaism—an idiosyncratic mix of Buddhism and Hinduism—chank shell is most conspicuous as a trumpet sounded in ceremonies. Sound figures prominently in Tibetan worship, during which drums, cymbals, wind instruments, bells, long metal trumpets, and chank shell trumpets supplement the human voice. Tibetans distinguish two kinds of shell trumpets: large shells, which produce a low tone, and small ones with a high-pitched note. The large shells often have a metal mount, which deepens their sound, heightening the contrast with the small trumpets. Priests, or lamas, kept large mounted chanks in the lamaseries, and blew them as a call to prayer and during important festivals, such as Buddha's birthday and New Year's ceremonies. These large chanks were always blown in pairs, of which one was considered male, the other female. Trumpet sound carried prayers spoken into the shells to the ears of a deity.

While Tibetans regarded the sound of the large chank

HINDU WOMAN POURING SACRED WATER FROM A CHANK SHELL

as auspicious, they considered the distinctive note of the small chank sad. Small chank trumpets were an essential part of funeral rituals. The funeral procession of even the poorest Tibetan would include at least one priest blowing a chank shell trumpet. Tibetans also put chank shells on altars as one of the offerings to the five senses; filled with curds, they were offered to the sense of smell. Chanks appear in Tibetan iconography as one of Buddhism's eight auspicious symbols.

In ancient Mexico, images of shells were common in pre-Columbian sculptures and paintings. Shell trumpets, usually made from the Horse Conch (*Pleuroploca gigantea*) or full-size ceramic replicas, are occasionally found in archaeological sites, but more frequently conchs and other shells are depicted in frescoes, codices, bas-reliefs, and on painted pots. Priests, and jaguars representing priests, are seen blowing shell trumpets, as in the famous fresco from the Palace of the Jaguars at Teotihuacán. Usually speech scrolls are shown emerging from the shells, suggesting either that the sound itself was a prayer or that the sound of the trumpet carried the priests' prayers to the ears of the gods.

In modern times the Huichol Indians of central Mexico still used a murex shell (*Murex nigritus*) during the most important ceremony of the annual ritual cycle: the feast of raw corn tamales. Once a year the Huichol bring the shell trumpet out of its hiding place in a ceremonial center. When the special tamales have been dedicated to the gods, the Indians blow the murex trumpet to signal the

PRE-COLUMBIAN CERAMIC POT, PERU

Conch shell trumpets were widespread in pre-Columbian Central and South America. This ceramic pot, modeled in the form of a figure blowing a shell trumpet, was made by the Moche people of northern Peru (0–A.D. 800).

deities that the sacred feast is ready. To the Huichol the markings on the murex shell symbolize water and kernels of corn, the two elements most important to their existence. The Huichol live far from the sea, but according to their traditions, nomadic Indians, the Chichimecas, brought them murex shells from the coast.

In Oaxaca, farther south, the olive shell *(Oliva porphyria)* is associated with the symbolic complex of rain, growth, and fertility. In the iconography of the Zapotec people of pre-Columbian Oaxaca, olive shell rattles are among the symbols associated with Cocijo, god of rain, and Xipe Totec, god of spring. On funerary urns representing these deities, all identifiable symbols on images of Cocijo—and many on Xipe Totec—refer to rain or water. Olive shell rattles turn up in archaeological excavations, but we could not find any suggestions for their use or meaning. However, an ethnographic account of modern Otomi ritual suggests a possible relationship between the shell rattles and rain. In a ceremony to bring rain, women carry digging sticks ordinarily used for planting crops, to which they have added a leather handle decorated with small bells. As the women dance, they strike the ground with the digging sticks and the bells tinkle. The ethnographer comments that at all times Mexico's farming peoples have relied on "the magic of sound" to bring rain, and he cites an ancient chant to Tlaloc, the rain god:

All day long we have made rain
In the courtyard of the temple.

PRE-COLUMBIAN FUNERARY URN, MEXICO

This ceramic funerary urn was made by the Zapotec people of Oaxaca, central Mexico, in the sixth or seventh century A.D. It represents Xipe Totec, god of spring. The Olive shells hanging from his belt appear to be symbolically associated with rain.

With the little mist rattles we have
Called to the water in the paradise of Tlaloc.

Since the olive shell rattles of the Zapotec appear in the context of rain symbols, the Indians may also have used the rattles to call forth rain from their rain god, Cocijo.

As in other arid regions of the world, this association of shell with rain, growth of crops, and fertility is a consistent theme in Mexican iconography. Another is the association of shells with birth and human fecundity. The conch shell—also called a sea snail—is the emblem of the goddess of the moon, who is linked with fertility and growth. The image of the sea snail can symbolize both the moon and the female sexual organs. One early commentator explained the analogy: "As the snail comes out of its shell, so man comes out of his mother's womb."

The two themes combine in the symbolism associated with Quetzalcoatl, the feathered serpent, one of the most important deities of the Aztec and pre-Aztec pantheon. Quetzalcoatl created all humankind from his own blood. He was the bearer of civilization: He brought the arts, metal-working, weaving, and corn. He was the god of the setting sun and the archetype of the priests (who blew the conch shell trumpets). As god of the wind he cleared the way for the rain gods to bring their clouds of fertilizing rain. Quetzalcoatl as portrayed in painting and sculpture usually wears a cross section of a conch shell as a pectoral ornament. Worshipers of Quetzalcoatl appear to have worn actual shells.

In the iconography of the ancient Maya of Mexico's

MAYA GOD EMERGES FROM A SHELL

These images of a god emerging from a conch shell are from paintings on Maya pottery.

Yucatan Peninsula, the association of shells with birth is more in evidence than association with rain and growth. When shells appear, they frequently have gods, human beings, or animallike creatures emerging from them. The Maya particularly associated the conch shell with Mam, the earth god, who is often depicted wearing a shell on his back or emerging from a shell. In an apparent contradiction, the conch shell was not only the Maya symbol of birth but also of the earth's interior, the world of death, darkness, and night. But from this realm birth takes place: Both human and plant life originated in the world of death. For the Maya, as for the Aztec, the symbol of the shell synthesized beliefs about birth and fertility, earth, rain, and growth.

QUETZALCOATL

In this painting of Quetzalcoatl from the Codex Borbonicus, an ancient parchment "book" containing drawings of myths, the god wears the cross section of shell as a pectoral ornament. Near his mouth there appears to be a speech scroll in the form of a conch shell.

EMBLEM OF THE GOD QUETZALCOATL

This cross section of a Horse Conch shell, emblem of the Aztec god Quetzalcoatl, was found in the Mexican state of Veracruz. The perforations indicate that it was worn perhaps by a priest or worshiper of Quetzalcoatl, or hung on an image of the god.

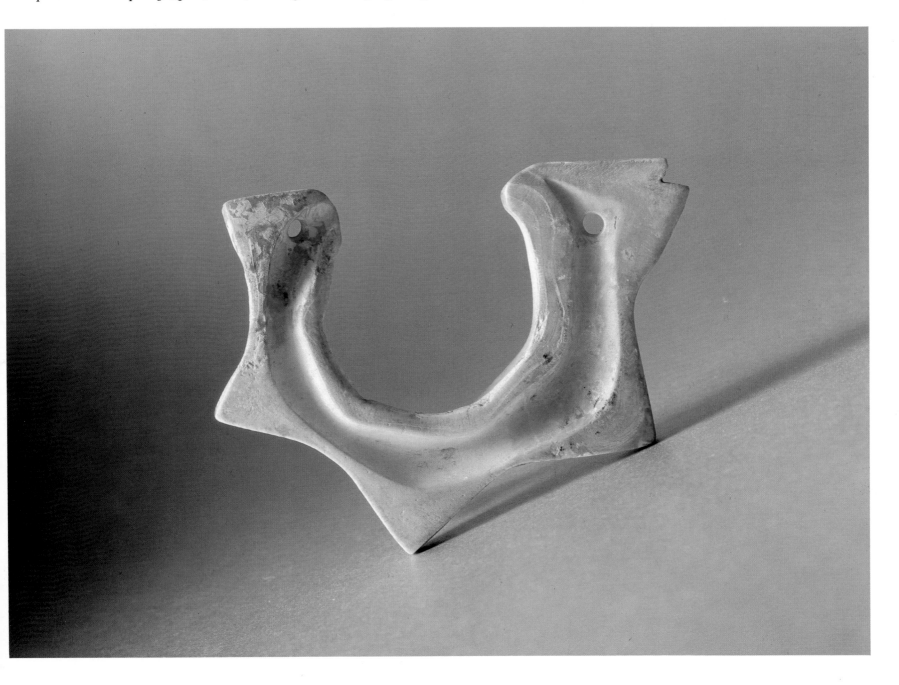

DETAIL: ZUNI FETISH NECKLACE

The shells and stone images of this necklace share an underlying theme. The butterfly is a Rain Being in Zuni myth. Another creature is probably a rattlesnake, judging by the markings at the end of its tail. In Pueblo rain ceremonies, the Indians appeal to rattlesnakes to intercede with rain clouds. The other identifiable image is a horned serpent, guardian of the sacred springs, closely associated with rain priests. Iridescent green pieces of abalone shell usually appear in the context of rain or sacred water. The preponderance of rain symbols suggests that this necklace was used during rain ceremonies.

NAVAHO MAN WEARING
FETISH NECKLACE

ZUNI KACHINA DOLL

This wooden Zuni kachina figure represents a corn maiden, a kachina (masked dancer) who dances at ceremonies to bring rain. The designs painted on the body represent rain clouds, falling rain, and butterflies, Rain Beings in Zuni myth. The step design in the headdress represents rain clouds, and the multicolored bands on the chin represent the rainbow. The band of squares across the forehead represents an ear of corn, the feathers at its ends, corn silk. The meaning of the piece of abalone shell hanging at the center of the forehead has not been reported, but abalone's consistent association with sacred water suggests that the pendant must symbolize the rain that makes the corn grow.

KACHINA DANCERS

159

PIPE, NORTH PACIFIC COAST, NORTH AMERICA

Facing page:

PIPE, NORTH PACIFIC COAST, NORTH AMERICA

*This carved wooden pipe bowl from the
Haida of British Columbia is in the form of
a cockle, from which, according to myth,
mankind was born. Raven, the creator, was
lonely and wanted a wife. In varying
versions, he either mated with a cockle or
otherwise caused tiny human beings, ancestors
of all Indians, to emerge from a shell. This
carving is particularly interesting because,
besides the cockle shell, it offers a fairly
accurate representation of the live mollusk
extending its siphon.*

BORNEO RATTLE

*The Dyak people of Borneo use this rattle of
basketry, land snails (Bertia brookei), and
freshwater snails (Pila ampulacea) to summon
spirits.*

CONGO FETISH FIGURE

This wooden fetish figure, made by the Bakete or Lulua people of Zaire, derives its power for both good and evil from the Giant Land Snail shell and the animal horn on its back, which contains magical medicines.

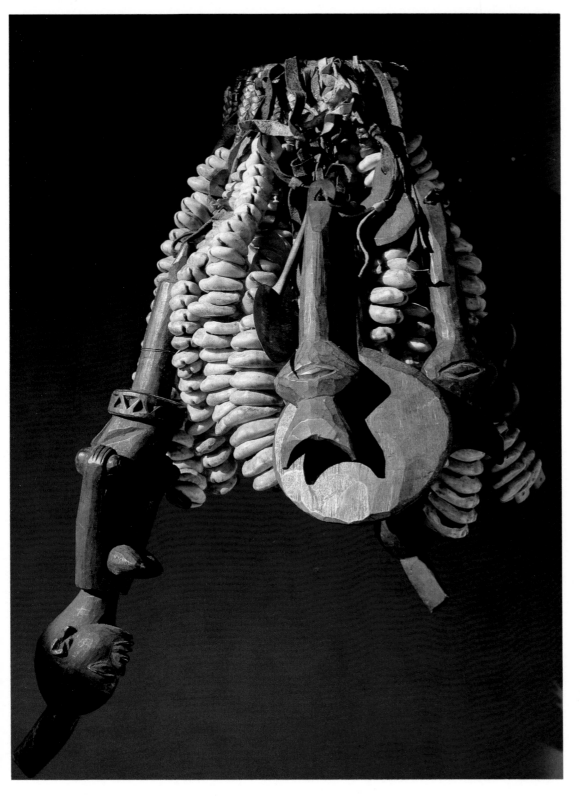

YORUBA RITUAL ORNAMENT, NIGERIA

Worshipers of the Yoruba god Elegba (also called Eshu) wear this ritual ornament composed of Ring Cowrie shells, wooden images of Elegba, and tin objects. The cowrie shells, traditional Yoruba money, refer to Elegba's role as protector of the marketplace and reflect his involvement in economic affairs.

YORUBA PRIESTESS, NIGERIA

OCEAN GODDESS NECKLACE, NIGERIA

Facing page:

OCEAN GODDESS NECKLACE, NIGERIA

Species of shells other than money and Ring Cowries appear on Yoruba ritual artifacts associated with river and ocean deities. These shells are usually marine or riverine shells native to the region. On this necklace of Olokun, goddess of the sea, the Money Cowries are joined by two large cowrie shells (Cypraea stercoraria) found off the Nigerian coast.

RITUAL FAN, WEST AFRICA

This fan of incised brass decorated with Money Cowrie shells dyed pale blue is carried by members of the Eleko cult, concerned with preventing death in children. Among the Yoruba of Nigeria, Money Cowries are symbolically associated with life-giving and curative powers.

DETAIL: WEST AFRICAN DANCE MASK

WEST AFRICAN DANCE MASK

People of many cultures have seen a resemblance between the cowrie shell and the human eye. Shells represent eyes on this mask of wood and raffia from the Bamileke people of the Cameroons.

NEW GUINEA FUNERARY MASK WITH
COWRIE SHELL EYES

This rare and possibly unique mask represents the spirit of a dead man at his funerary ceremony. Collected in the nineteenth century from somewhere along the Sepik River, it is made of barkcloth decorated with Nassa shells (Nassarius sp.), cowrie shells, and a piece of baler shell (Melo sp.). During funeral ceremonies a man would appear under cover of darkness wearing a mask like this one representing the ghost of the deceased. After a ceremony placating the ghost, the mask was hidden in a special place in the forest, away from the village, so that the ghost could not find its way back to harm villagers. The cowrie shells represent closed eyes; the eyes of these masks are always closed so that the ghost cannot see and harm the living.

SHELL RATTLES AND TRUMPETS

Clockwise: (1) Philippine tinkler of Windowpane shell to keep away evil spirits. (2) A rattle of scallop shells used in curing by Tlingit shamans of Alaska. (3) An ankle rattle of cockle shells worn during dances by Andaman Islanders. (4) Shell-shaped clay whistle, pre-Columbian Ecuador. (5) Pre-Columbian shell whistle from Peru. (6) Shell-shaped clay whistle, pre-Columbian Peru. (7) An incised Chank shell trumpet from India. (8) A Triton's Trumpet from New Britain, Melanesia.

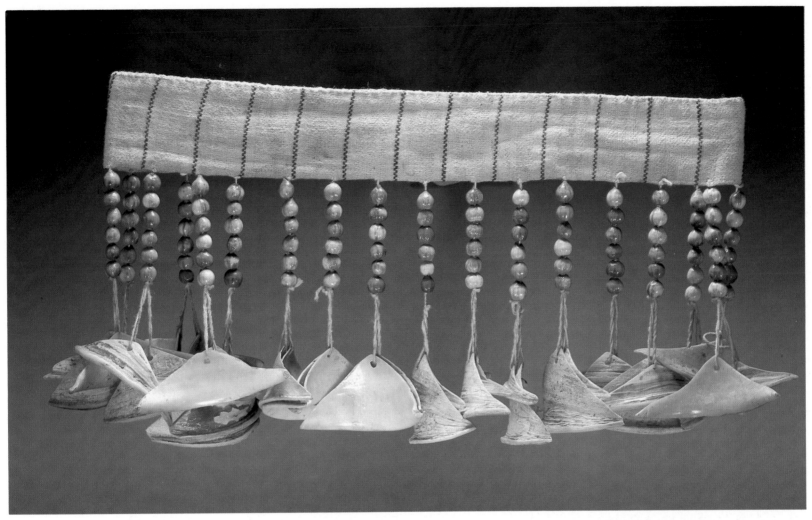

JIVARO DANCE BELT, ECUADOR

JIVARO WOMAN WEARING DANCE BELT

YUROK GIRL WEARING
DANCE SKIRT

DANCE SKIRT, OREGON (USA)

SHASTA SHAMAN'S BELT MADE WITH
HUMAN HAIR AND PALE ABALONE
DISCS, NORTHERN CALIFORNIA

CONE SHELL BRACELETS, PHILIPPINES

BAGOBO GIRL WEARING
SHELL BRACELET

FUNERARY STICK, SOLOMON ISLANDS

These ritual objects, made of cut cone shells and auger shells, were kept together with skulls of dead ancestors in small funerary houses. The shells represent spirits of dead chiefs and were used by living chiefs to communicate with their dead ancestors, either to placate them or to seek their aid. When the Islanders went on head-hunting raids, they attached such sticks to their canoes, thus carrying along with them the spirits of the chiefs to attract enemy skulls.

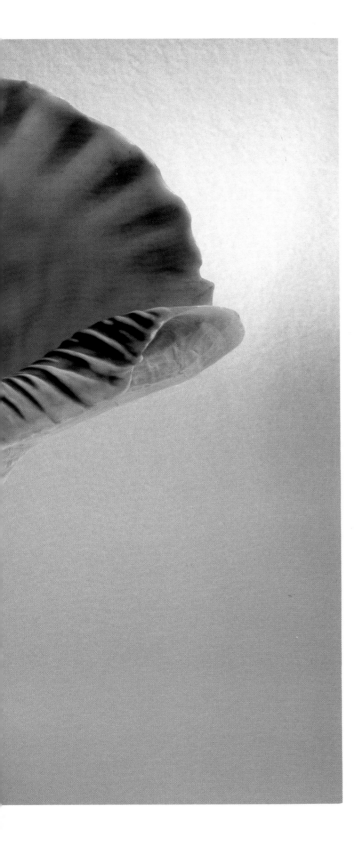

PRIEST'S TRUMPET, JAPAN

In Japan a shell trumpet appears as the emblem of the Yamabushi, priests of an ascetic Buddhist sect called Shugendo. The Yamabushi worship sacred mountains in order to acquire magical powers over evil and perform ceremonies to bring good harvests, to exorcise evil spirits from houses and villages, and to offer prayers for the sick. Each priest carries a Triton's Trumpet with brass mouthpiece hanging from his waist by a silk cord. This shell trumpet communicates both with the spirits' world and with human participants. In the mountains, priests signal other groups with their shell trumpets; all Shugendo ceremonies begin with the sounding of the Triton's Trumpet. In a ceremony representing symbolic birth, the shell trumpet's note signifies the sound of the opening of the gate from the world of the sacred so that birth into the natural world may take place.

FIJIAN BLOWING TRITON'S TRUMPET

DETAIL: CEREMONIAL TRUMPET, TIBET

CEREMONIAL TRUMPET, TIBET

This rare and beautiful example of a Tibetan Chank shell trumpet is mounted with bronze and copper decorated with elaborate designs of dragons, deities, and other symbols, and studded with turquoise and coral. The inscription on the back reads: "In K——— during the time of Kurtimurti. Water Snake year [A.D. 1400]."

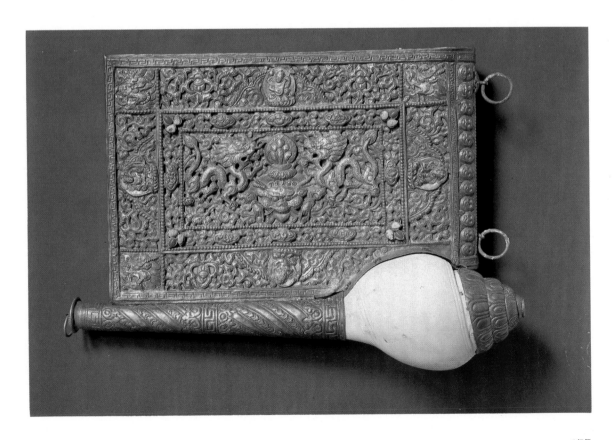

PRE-COLUMBIAN CONCH SHELL TRUMPET, MEXICO

This pre-Columbian Horse Conch trumpet was probably excavated in the highlands of central Mexico. The unusual decoration, a thick layer of paint applied to the surface, areas cut away and filled with paints of other colors, has been called paint cloisonné.

DETAIL: PRE-COLUMBIAN CONCH SHELL TRUMPET, MEXICO

CHINESE ROD PUPPET

HEAD OF A CHINESE ROD PUPPET

The conch shell painted on the face of this rod puppet identifies it as the Spirit of Conch Shell, a sea spirit in a traditional puppet play, The White Snake. In Chinese folklore the spirit who lives within the conch shell controls weather and protects against the sea's dangers. One account describes a Chinese emperor taking a large white conch shell to the sea on important occasions to ensure good weather. Another story tells of a rare, left-handed Chank shell loaned to important persons departing on a sea voyage. The Chinese believed that if the storm spirits living in the shell were well treated, they would either bring good weather or give storm warnings well in advance. A similar Tibetan belief decreed that every sailor had to carry a conch shell to frighten away the mythical sea dragon that overturns ships.

Notes

Where information about a group exists in standard or readily available sources, I refer the reader to my principal sources, particularly those with extensive bibliographies. Where specific data about the use or significance of shells is easily accessible in these sources, I have not gone into more detail. Where there are many such sources, I do give the source of specific information. For general information, as well as specific data on shells, which comes from obscure or unpublished sources, both the information in the text and the references cited are more detailed. In most cases a great deal of material has been compressed into a few paragraphs or even a few sentences in the text, and it is hoped that interested readers will use the listed sources to pursue the subjects further. When no source is cited for information about an artifact, the information comes from the American Museum of Natural History (AMNH) catalogs. (The letter c. following page number indicates reference to caption.)

Introduction

Page 9: **Shell analogies in European literature:** Bachelard.

Shells in daily life

For information on the biology of mollusks throughout the chapter, I have relied primarily on William Emerson, 1972, and personal communication. For general information about the use of shells I found Abbott, 1954 and 1972, and Jackson most reliable and useful (although Jackson is considerably out of date).

Page 19–20: **Role of mollusks in the evolution of human society.** Bailey, Binford and Binford, Flannery, Meighen, Shackleton, Ucko and Dimbleby. Also Junius Bird and David Hurst Thomas, personal communications. Opinions differ whether increased population resulted from the appearance of new food resources or whether increased population was the cause that led to a search for new resources.
Page 20: **Snail cultivation in Nigeria:** *The New Scientist,* May 9, 1974. **Historical information about food:** Tannahill (food of the poor, oysters), Brothwell and Brothwell, Evans, 1969 (*World Archaeology*—snails), Greengo (U.S. West Coast), Ucko and Dimbleby. **Snails in Ghana:** Enid Schildkrout, personal communication.
Page 21ff.: **Shells and archaeology, general:** Evans (*World Archaeology,* 1969), Heizer (1960), Meighen, Michels, Shackleton. **Midden analysis:**
Biggs, Heizer (1958), Meighen, Meighen et al., Shackleton.
Page 22ff.: **Japanese middens:** Groot, Groot and Sinoto, Kidder, Morse.
Page 22c.: **Model of Japanese midden:** based on Kidder.
Page 23: **Early archaeology:** Daniel, Lubbock, Morse.
Page 24: **Daily growth rings:** Bailey, Coutts, Koike, Weide.
Page 25: **Land snails:** Baker, Evans (*World Archaeology,* 1969), Sparks. **Trade routes:** See *World Archaeology* 5, no. 2 (1973): special issue on trade; Clark, Poulsen, Tower, Winters.
Page 26ff.: **Shellfish dye, general:** Abbott, 1954 and 1972. **Tyrian Purple:** Born, Forbes (process), Schunk, Singer et al. **Silk trade:** Boulnois; Hudson (p. 96) notes that according to a Chinese source textiles from the regions we now call Egypt and Syria were superior in color. This would appear to refer to purple-dyed cloth.
Page 26c.: **Hopewell:** Prufer, Silverberg (excellent bibliography).
Page 28: **Purple in the Old Testament and the Talmud:** Rabbi Chaim Gold of New York City generously shared his unpublished work on the dyes mentioned in the Old Testament and its commentaries (see Exodus, chapters 25–28, and Ezekiel, chapter 27), and supplied us with translations of references in the Talmud and Midrash. Also Rubens. **Ireland:** Jackson. **Purple in the Middle Ages:** Roosen-Runge, Roosen-Runge and Werner, Smith and Hawthorne. **Asia:** Minnich (identifies royal purple in Japan as coming from vegetable sources), Reischauer. For information about modern Japan we are grateful to Nabuko Kajatani of the Metropolitan Museum of Art for both information and translations from Japanese sources.
Page 29: **Purple in Peru:** Saltzman et al.; Junius Bird, personal communication. **Purple in Mexico:** Gerhard (1964a, 1964b), Nuttall. **Shell lime in New England:** Wood. **As temper:** Matson, Shepard. **As paint:** e.g., Blackwood. **In glue:** Laguna.
Page 31: In the photograph the axe held by this New Guinea man appears to be made of shell, but it could be stone.
Page 32: **Sumerian lamps:** Wooley. **Balinese lamps:** Kleiweg de Zwaan. **Florida tools:** Goggin, Griffin, Knight, Moore, Rau, Rouse, Webster.
Page 33c.: **Shell ring manufacture:** Gardi (1958, 1960).
Page 34: **Tuamotu:** Emory.
Page 35: The brown designs of the Akawaio discs were identified as periostricum by Harold Feinberg, dept. of invertebrates, AMNH. **Akawaio:** Roth, in Thurm.
Page 36: **Fishhooks:** Anell, Beasley, Bird and Bennett (Chile), Curtis, Edward W. Gifford, Laxson, David Rogers.
Page 47c.: **Octopus lure:** Ellis, Hornell (1950), Frank Lane.

Shells as wealth

Economic anthropology is a subject rife with controversies. My basic reading on the theoretical bases of the subject included: Bohannan and Dalton, Cohen, Dalton, Firth (1967), Firth and Yamey, Frankenberg, Herskovits (1952), Melitz, Polanyi, Sahlins, Salisbury (1973). Works specifically devoted to the topic of money were Einzig, Quiggen, Stearns, Bronson, Chagnon.

Page 50: **Cowrie shell money in China and India:** Egami (China—excellent). Also Andersson, Lacouperie, Gibson, Jackson, Wang.

Page 50c.: **Devaluation of cowrie shells in New Guinea:** Hughes. **Kakoli:** AMNH accession notes.

Page 51: **Cowrie shell money in Africa:** Johnson. Also Bovill, Grey and Birmingham, Hiskett, Morton-Williams (1969), Posnansky.

Page 52: **Cowrie shell values:** Skinner (Mossi, citing Tauxier), Vansina (1962—Kuba), Johnson (Bambara, citing Mungo Park).

Page 53ff.: **Dentalia among Yurok and Tolowa:** Chagnon, Drucker (1965), Gould (1966).

Page 53c.: **Wampum:** Beauchamps, Douglas and Jeancon, Snyderman, Speck.

Page 57: **Dentalia values:** Kroeber (1925).

Page 57ff.: **Pomo shell beads:** Barrett (1908, 1917, 1952), Edward Curtis.

Page 58: **Bead values:** Loeb.

Page 59ff.: **General purpose and limited purpose money:** See Dalton, Polanyi, and other economic theorists mentioned at beginning of section.

Page 59c.: **Pump drills:** McGuire. **Cochiti shell values:** Lange.

Page 61ff.: **Shells in New Guinea, general:** Hughes. **Chambri:** Mead (1935, 1938). **Tsembaga:** Rappoport.

Page 64: **Mount Hagen Moka:** Andrew Strathern (1971), Marilyn Strathern (1972), Strathern and Strathern. Also Brown, Elkin, Glasse and Meggitt, Meggitt.

Page 66: **Tolai:** Epstein, Salisbury (1970).

Page 69: **Baegu:** Ross. **Kula ring:** Malinowski. Also Cranstone; Mauss, Uberoi.

Page 70: **Cone shell discs in southern and south central Africa** are also called *mpande, andoro, vibangwa.* See p. 97ff for further discussion and references.

Page 71c.: **Abalone shell:** Boas (1896), Caamano (1846—quoted by Gunther, 1972), Drucker (1965), Gunther (1966, 1972), Harner and Essler. The chief's daughter is the wife of George Hunt, Boas's chief assistant (according to note with photograph).

Page 73: In the photograph the pipe represents a killer whale or Orca.

Page 74c.: **Spondylus trade in South America:** Paulsen. Also Lathrap (1973, 1975), Murra.

Page 75c.: **Burmese ornament:** F. K. Lehmann (notes to AMNH collection and 1963).

Shells as emblems of status

Page 77c.: Heizer and Whipple, Kroeber (1925).

Page 78c.: Halpern (quote—p. 59), Kroeber, Loeb.

Page 80c.: **Tsembaga:** Rappoport.

Page 81c.: **Chambri:** Mead (1935, 1938).

Page 83c.: Murra.

Page 86c.: **Chambri (married women not wearing shells):** Robin Hide (Ogden Mills Fellow, AMNH), personal communication.

Page 86c., 87: **Turkana:** Herbert Cole, Gulliver (1953). Also Adamson, Emley, Gulliver (1955).

Page 88: **Arapesh:** Mead (1935: 74; 1940: 420).

Page 88c.: **Kalash women:** Quentric, Rajput. **Waigal Valley:** Jones.

Page 90: **Hindu married women:** Hornell (1916, 1942). **Chank bracelet in Nepal and Bhutan:** Hildburgh (1909 and notes to AMNH collections).

Page 91: **Andaman Islands:** Radcliffe-Brown. My interpretation of his data.

Page 93c.: **Chambri and Iatmul skulls:** Newton, Margaret Mead (notes to AMNH collections). Mr. Korwa, director, West Irian Museum (personal communication) and Deborah Gewertz, Amherst College (personal communication) concur that cowrie shells signify wealth. Rhoda Metraux, AMNH, disagrees.

Page 94ff.: **Kuba:** Vansina (1955, 1958, 1959, 1964), Torday and Joyce, Willett. Also Harroy, Starr.

Page 97: **Cone shell discs in Africa:** Livingstone, Harding, Miracle.

Page 98: **Ba-Ila:** Smith and Dale. **Vahumbe:** Delachaux and Thiebaud. Also Laszlo. According to Mary Douglas (personal communication), among the Lele of the Kasai the cone shell was so sacred that she was never permitted to see it.

Page 99: **Fiji:** Hocart (1929), Laura Thompson. **Golden cowrie:** Erskine, Charles Hunt, director, Fiji Museum (personal communication).

Page 100c., 101: **Kaps-kaps: New Ireland:** Phillip Gifford and Dorothy Billings (personal communications). **Solomons:** Ross. **Breastplate:** Barrow, Deane, Hocart (1929), Quain, Rougier, Laura Thompson.

Page 102: **Shells in ancient China:** cited by Egami.

Page 103c.: **Egg shells in Manus:** Mead (1934 and personal communication). Also Buhler et al., Fortune.

Page 104: **Nagas:** Elwin, Fürer-Haimendorf, Hodson, Hutton. **Drawing:** Butler.

Page 105: **Haka Chin:** Lehmann (1963, and notes to AMNH collection). Also Parry. **Waigal Valley:** Schuyler Jones (personal communication).

Page 105ff.: **Taiwan:** Primary source for costume and ornament: Chen Chi-lu. **Tribal peoples of Taiwan, general:** Ferrell, Mackay, Mabuchi, McGovern.

Page 106: **Atayal:** Ho Ting Jui (1953, 1954), Ruey Yih-fu. **Paiwan:** Li Yih-Yuan, Wei Hwei-lin (1955). **Bunun:** McGovern, Michael Coe (notes to AMNH collections). Tang Mei-chun, Visiting Professor at Columbia University, supplied us with unpublished information and translated articles from Chinese.

Page 108: **Philippines tribes, general:** Kroeber (1928), Zamora. **Igorot and Kalinga:** Dozier, Eggan, Folkmar, Jenks, Scott, Vanoverbergh, Worcester, Michiko Takaki, University of Massachusetts, personal communication (significance of shell disc among the Kalinga).

Page 110: **Galla:** Haberland, Huntingford, Lewis.

Page 113c.: **Bambara Ntomo ritual:** Imperato (1975 and personal communication).

Page 116c.: **Bagobo and neighboring tribes:** Laura Benedict (1916 and notes to AMNH collections). Also Fay Cooper Cole (1911, 1913, 1956),

Garvan (1927, 1931).

Page 119c.: **Lime spatula:** Rhoda Metraux (AMNH) and Mr. Korwa (director, West Irian Museum), personal communications.

Shells in ritual and myth

Ritual and symbolism is the area of my strongest personal interest. My thinking has been influenced primarily by my teachers Rodney Needham and E. E. Evans-Pritchard and by the writings of Edmund Leach, Victor Turner, and Claude Levi-Strauss.

Page 121ff.: **African land snail: Lunda:** Reynolds, Fisher. **Lulua:** Fourche and Morlighen (1937, 1939). **Luba:** Burton, Torday and Joyce. Also Colle. **Other tribes:** DeJonghe, Koulaseli (detailed ethnography about animal horns).

Page 123ff.: **Basic works on aborigines, especially ritual:** Berndt and Berndt (1964; also 1943), Kaberry, Tindale. **Pitjantjara:** Gould (1969, notes to AMNH collections, and personal communication). **Jigalog:** Robert Tonkinson, personal communication. Special thanks to Richard Gould and Robert Tonkinson for extensive personal communications.

Page 126ff.: **Pueblos:** Most comprehensive work is Parsons (1939). Also Ruth Benedict, Bunzel, Parsons (1933).

Page 127: **Big shell (several versions of myth):** Cushing (1896), Parsons (1933, 1939), Stephen. **Gathering shells at the Pacific:** Woodward.

Page 129: **War gods:** Parsons (1918, 1939).

Page 129c.: **Hunters' fetishes:** Cushing (1883), Parsons (1939).

Page 130: **Abalone:** Parsons (1939), Stevenson (1894).

Page 133ff.: **Yoruba:** Bascom (basic; good bibliography), Challenor (smallpox), Frobenius (detailed early ethnography), Herskovits (Shopona), Lucas, Morton-Williams (1964, 1969), Ojo, Robert Thompson (1973, 1976—symbolism, iconography), Verger, Westcott, and Morton-Williams. **Cowrie trade:** Johnson, Hiskett.

Page 133c.: **Plains Indians, clamshell disc:** Wissler. Also Mails.

Page 137: **Bini:** Ben-Amos (symbolism of white gods).

Page 139: **Andaman Islands:** Radcliffe-Brown.

Page 139c.: **Highland New Guinea, Melpa:** Strathern and Strathern, Andrew Strathern (1971 and personal communication).

Page 140: **Evil eye, general:** Elworthy, Maloney. **Middle East:** Spooner, Edward Lane (Egypt). **India:** Crooke. In south, Indian domestic animals, particularly bullocks, wear cowrie shell garlands as protective amulets, but it is not clear that the evil eye concept is present. **Europe:** Hildburgh (1942). **Antiquity:** Strabo, vol. 7, para. 17. **Pomo:** Loeb. **Saha shell offerings:** Jane Safer, unpublished.

Page 141c.: **Bagobo bracelet:** Laura Benedict.

Page 142: **Desana:** Reichel-Dolmatoff. **Kaatans:** Bastien.

Page 143ff.: **Sound:** Needham. Except for this article by Needham the significance of sound in ritual has been largely unexplored.

Page 144: **Jivaro:** Harner, Karsten. "Appears to play an essential role" is my inference from Harner and Karsten's data.

Page 147: **Shamans' rattles:** Drucker (1955). In the AMNH Emmons collection of Northwest Coast artifacts all the scallop shell rattles are specifically identified as belonging to shamans. We could not find any photographs of a shell rattle being used. **Philippines shell tinkler:** Frederick Starr, AMNH catalog.

Page 147c.: **Hupa and Yurok:** Gifford and Kroeber, Kroeber (1925).

Page 148: **Trumpets: Fiji:** Hocart (1929), Larsson. **Eddystone:** Hocart (1935; also 1922). **Chank shell in India:** Information about the sacred chank is in all standard works on Indian ritual and symbol. Hornell (1916) is devoted totally to the chank. The spiral character of Vishnu symbols is suggested by Beck.

Page 150: **Tibet:** Olson (excellent catalog), also Waddell (quoted in AMNH notes to collections). For information about the pairs of chank shell trumpets and the distinction between funeral and festival trumpets, we are grateful to Sonam Paljor Densongpa of Sikkim.

Page 152: **Ifugao**—Barton (1946). Also Barton (1922), Lambrecht (1955), Worcester. **Pre-Columbian trumpets: Teotihuacan**—Miller (1973 and personal communication); **Oaxaca:** Boos, Caso, Neumann. In researching both photographs and urns in AMNH collections, we found pendant olive shells only in the context of images of Cocijo and Xipe Totec.

Page 153: **Otomi and chant to Tlaloc:** Soustelle.

Page 154c.: **Birth from shell: Mexico**—Images of people, gods, or fantastic creatures emerging from shells are common throughout ancient Mexican and Mayan iconography; e.g., Teotihuacan (Miller), various codices, Mayan frescoes and painted pots.

Page 155: **Shells in Mexican iconography:** Miller, Kubler, Sejourne (1956, 1962), Simoni, Westheim. Sahagun and Pedro de Rios quoted in Sejourne. Also Codex Borgia.

Page 156: **Mayan iconography:** J.E.S. Thompson. In Mayan hieroglyphics the glyph for zero is a snail.

Page 158c.: **Rain symbols:** Ruth Benedict, Fewkes (1910), Parsons (1939).

Page 159c.: **Kachinas:** Bunzel, Fewkes (1897, 1903), Parsons (1939), Stevenson (1904).

Page 161c.: **Northwest Coast:** Barbeau, Deans, Niblack, West.

Page 162c.: **Congo fetish:** see p. 121ff.

Page 163c.: **Yoruba:** see p. 133ff.

Page 164c.: **Yoruba:** see p. 133ff.

Page 165c.: **Yoruba:** see p. 133ff.

Page 167c.: **New Guinea funerary mask:** Mr. Korwa, director, West Irian Museum (personal communication).

Page 173: **Funerary stick:** Hocart (1922), Barraud.

Page 175c.: **Japanese trumpet:** Earhart, Richard Leavitt (personal communication).

Page 178c.: **Painted trumpet**—Gordon Ekholm (personal communication).

Page 180c.: **Chinese puppet:** For information about the conch shell spirit puppet I am grateful to Betty Erda (AMNH). This information comes from untranslated notes to collection by B. Laufer. **Chinese folk tales:** Rockhill, and supplementary notes in *Journal of the North China Branch, Royal Asiatic Society* 3:20. The Tibetan myth was told to us by Sonam Paljor Densongpa.

Bibliography

Abbott, Robert Tucker. *American Seashells*. New York, 1954.
———. *Kingdom of the Seashell*. New York, 1972.
Adamson, Joy. *Peoples of Kenya*. London, 1967.
Andersson, J. Gunnar. *Children of the Yellow Earth; Studies in Prehistoric China*. London, 1934.
Anell, Bengt. *Contribution to the History of Fishing in the South Seas*. Stockholm, 1955.
Bachelard, Gaston. *The Poetics of Space*. Translated by Maria Jolas. Boston, 1969.
Bailey, G. N. "The role of molluscs in coastal economies: the results of midden analysis in Australia." *Journal of Archaeological Science* 2 (1975).
Baker, Frank Collins. "Pleistocene land and freshwater mollusca as indicators of time and ecological conditions." In *Early Man*, edited by G. G. MacCurdy. Philadelphia, 1937.
Barbeau, Marius. "Haida myths illustrated in argillite carvings." *National Museum of Canada Bulletin*, no. 127 (1953), Ottowa.
Baric, Lorraine. "Some aspects of credit, saving, and investment in a nonmonetary economy." In Firth and Yamey.
Barraud, C. , "De la chasse aux têtes à la peche à la bonite." *l'Homme*, vol. 12, no. 1, 1972.
Barrett, Samuel Alfred. "Ceremonies of the Pomo Indians." *University of California Publications in American Archaeology and Ethnology*, vol. 12, no. 10. Berkeley, 1917.
———. "Material aspects of Pomo culture." *Bulletin of the Public Museum of the City of Milwaukee* 20, parts 1 and 2. 1952.
———. "Pomo Indian basketry." *University of California Publications in American Archaeology and Ethnology*, vol. 7, no. 3. Berkeley, 1908.
Barrow, Terence T. *Art and Life in Polynesia*. Rutland, Vermont, and Tokyo, 1972.
Barton, Roy Franklin. "Ifugao economics." *University of California Publications in American Archaeology and Ethnology*, vol. 15, no. 5. Berkeley, 1922.
———. *The Religion of the Ifugaos*. Memoirs of the American Anthropological Association, no. 65 (1946).
Bascom, William Russell. *The Yoruba of Southwestern Nigeria*. New York, 1969.
Bastien, Joseph. *Mountain of the Condor: metaphor and ritual in an Andean ayllu*. American Ethnological Society Monograph, no. 64. St. Paul, 1978.
Beasley, Harry G. *Pacific Island Records: Fishhooks*. London, 1928.
Beauchamps, William M. "Wampum and shell articles used by the New York Indians." *Bulletin of the New York State Museum* 8, no. 41 (1901).
Beck, Brenda. "Saiva/Vaisnava contrasts in Hindu mythology." Paper presented at the Learned Societies meetings, Toronto, 1974.

Ben-Amos, Paula. "Symbolism in Olokun mud art." *African Arts* 6, no. 4 (1973).
Benedict, Laura W. "A study of Bagobo ceremonial, magic and myth." *Annals of the New York Academy of Sciences*, vol. 25. New York, 1916.
Benedict, Ruth. *Zuni Mythology*. Columbia University Contributions to Anthropology, vol. 21, 2 parts. New York, 1935.
Berndt, Ronald M., and Berndt, Catherine. "A preliminary report of field work in the Ooldea region, western South Australia." *Oceania* 14, 4 parts (1943).
———. *The World of the First Australians*. Chicago, 1964.
Biggs, H. E. J. "Molluscs from human habitation sites and the problem of ethnological interpretation." In *Science in Archeology*, edited by D. Brothwell and E. Higgs. New York, 1970.
Binford, L. R., and Binford, S. R., ed. *New Perspectives in Archeology*. Chicago, 1968.
Bird, Junius, and Bennett, Wendell. *Andean Culture History*. American Museum of Natural History Handbook, no. 15. New York, 1949.
Blackwood, Beatrice. *Both Sides of Buka Passage*. Oxford, 1935.
Boas, Franz. "The social organization and the secret societies of the Kwakiutl Indians. *Report of the U.S. National Museum for 1891–92*, published 1896.
Bohannan, Paul, and Dalton, George, eds. *Markets in Africa*. Evanston, 1962.
Boos, Frank H. *The Ceramic Sculptures of Ancient Oaxaca*. London, 1966.
Born, Wolfgang. "Purpura shellfish," "Purple in classical antiquity," "Purple in the Middle Ages," "The use of purple among the Indians of Central America." *Ciba Review*, no. 4 (1937), Basel, Switzerland.
Boulnois, Luce. *The Silk Road*. New York, 1966.
Bourke, John G. *The Snake-Dance of the Moquis of Arizona*. New York, 1884.
Bovill, E. W. *Caravans of the Old Sahara*. London, 1933.
Bronson, Bennet. "Cash, cannon, and cowrie shells: the non-modern moneys of the world." *Field Museum of Natural History Bulletin* 47, no. 10 (1976).
Brothwell, Don, and Brothwell, Patricia. *Food in Antiquity*. New York, 1969.
Brown, Paula. "*Mingge*-money: economic change in the New Guinea highlands." *Southwestern Journal of Anthropology* 26 (1970).
Buhler, Alfred; Barrow, Terence; and Mountford, Charles P. *The Art of the South Sea Islands*. New York, 1962.
Bunzel, Ruth. "Introduction to Zuni ceremonialism." *Bureau of American Ethnology Annual Report for 1929–30*, published 1932.
Burton, William F. "Luba religion and magic in custom and belief." *Annales de Musee Royal de l'Afrique Centrale*, no. 35. Tervuren, Belgium, 1961.
Butler, John. *Travels and Adventures in the Province of Assam*. London, 1855.
Caso, Alfonso, and Bernal, Ignacio. *Urnas de Oaxaca*. Mexico City, 1952.
Chagnon, Napoleon. "Ecological and adaptive aspects of California shell money." *Archaeological Survey Annual Report*. UCLA Anthropology Dept., 1970.
Challenor, Bernard D. "Cultural resistance to smallpox vaccination in West Africa." *Journal of Tropical Medicine and Hygiene* 74 (1971).
Chen Chi-lu. *Material Culture of the Formosan Aborigines*. Taipei, 1968.
Cipriani, Lidio. *The Andaman Islanders*. Translated by D. Tayler Cox. New York, 1966.

Clark, J. G. D. *Prehistoric Europe: the economic basis.* London, 1952.

Cohen, Percy S. "Economic analysis and economic man: some comments on a controversy." In *Themes in Economic Anthropology,* Association of Social Anthropologists Monograph, no. 6, edited by Raymond Firth. London, 1967.

Cole, Fay Cooper. "The Bagobos of Davao Gulf." *Philippine Journal of Science* 6, no. 3 (1911).

——. "The Bukidnon of Mindinao." *Fieldiana.* Anthropology, vol. 46. Chicago, 1956.

——. "The wild tribes of the Davao District, Mindinao." *Field Museum of Natural History Publication* 170. Anthropology, vol. 12, no. 2 (1913).

Cole, Herbert M. "Vital arts in northern Kenya." *African Arts* 7, no. 2 (winter 1974).

Colle, le R. P. *Les Baluba (Congo Belge).* 2 vols. Brussels, 1913.

Coutts, P. J. F. "Bivalve-growth patterning as a method for seasonal dating in archaeology." *Nature* 226 (30 May 1970).

Crane, Louise. *China in sign and symbol.* London, 1927.

Cranstone, B. A. L. *Melanesia: a short ethnography.* British Museum, London, 1961.

Crooke, W. *An Introduction to Popular religion and folk-lore of northern India.* Allahabad, 1894.

Curtis, Edward S. *The North American Indian,* vol. 14. New York, 1924.

Curtis, Freddie. "Shell fishhooks of Indians of southern California." *Hawaiian Shell News,* September 1966.

Cushing, Frank H. "Outlines of Zuni creation." *U.S. Bureau of Ethnology Annual Report for 1892–93,* published 1896.

——. "Zuni fetishes." *U.S. Bureau of Ethnology Annual Report for 1880–81,* published 1883.

Dalton, George. *Economic Anthropology and Development.* New York, 1971.

Daniel, Glyn. *The Origins and Growth of Archaeology.* New York, 1967.

Deane, Wallace. *Fijian Society.* London, 1921.

Deans, James. "The Hidery story of creation." *American Antiquarian* 17, no. 2 (1895).

DeJonghe, M. E. "Les arbres-a-esprits au Kasai." *Bulletin des seances de l'Institut Royal Colonial Belge,* 8 (1937).

Delachaux, Theodore, and Thiebaud, Charles. *Land und Volker von Angola.* Nuremberg, 1936.

Dixon, R. B. "Basketry designs of the Indians of northern California." *Bulletin of the American Museum of Natural History* 17 (1902).

Douglas, F. H., and Jeancon, J. A. "Iroquoian and Algonkin wampum." Denver Art Museum, Indian leaflet series, no. 31 (1931): 1–4.

Dozier, Edward. *The Kalinga of Northern Luzon.* New York, 1967.

Drucker, Philip. *Cultures of the North Pacific Coast.* San Francisco, 1965.

——. *Indians of the Northwest Coast.* New York: American Museum of Natural History, 1955.

Earhart, H. Byron. *A Religious Study of the Mount Haguro Sect of Shugendo.* Sophia University Press, Tokyo, 1970.

Egami, Namio. "Migration of cowrie-shell culture in East Asia." *Acta Asiatica,* no. 26 (1974), Tokyo.

Eggan, Fred. "The Sagada Igorots of northern Luzon." In *Social Structure in Southeast Asia,* edited by George P. Murdock. Wenner-Gren Foundation Publication no. 29. New York, 1960.

Einzig, Paul. *Primitive Money.* London, 1949.

Eitel, Dr. "Les Hak-ka." *L'Anthropologie,* tome 4, Paris, 1893.

Elkin, A. P. "Delayed exchange in Wabag sub-district, Central Highlands of New Guinea." *Oceania* 23, no. 3 (1953).

Ellis, William. *Polynesian Researches,* 2nd ed. London, 1831.

Elwin, Verrier. *Nagas in the Nineteenth Century.* London, 1909.

Elworthy, Frederick T. *The Evil Eye: its origins and practices of superstition.* New York, 1958.

Emerson, William K. *Shells.* New York, 1972.

Emley, E. "The Turkana of Kolosia District." *Journal of the Royal Anthropological Society* 57 (1927).

Emory, Kenneth. "Material Culture of Tuamoto Archipelago." *Pacific Anthropological Records,* no. 22 (1975). Bernice P. Bishop Museum, Honolulu.

Epstein, A. L. "Tambu—a primitive shell money." *Discovery* 24 (December 1963).

Erskine, John. *Journal of a Cruise among the Islands of the Western Pacific.* London, 1853.

Evans, J. G. "The exploitation of molluscs." In Ucko and Dimbleby, eds.

——. "Land and freshwater mollusca in archaeology: chronological aspects." *World Archaeology* 1, no. 2 (1969).

——. *Land Snails in Archaeology.* London, 1972.

Ferrell, Raleigh. *Taiwan Aboriginal Groups.* Academia Sinica. Institute of Ethnology Monograph, no. 17. Taipei, 1969.

Fewkes, J. W. "The butterfly in Hopi myth and ritual." *American Anthropology* 12, no. 4 (1910).

——. "Hopi katcinas drawn by native artists." *U.S. Bureau of American Ethnology Annual Report for 1899–1900,* published 1903.

——. "Tusayan katcinas." *U.S. Bureau of American Ethnology Annual Report for 1893–94,* published 1897.

Firth, Raymond, ed. *Themes in Economic Anthropology.* Association of Social Anthropologists Monograph, no. 6. London, 1967. (Also Firth's article of same name in same source.)

——, and Yamey, B. S., eds. *Capital, Saving and Credit in Peasant Societies.* Chicago, 1964.

Fisher, W. Singleton. "Black magic feuds." *African Studies* 8, no.1 (1949), Johannesburg.

Flannery, Kent V. "Origins and ecological effects of early domestication in Iran and the Near East." In Ucko and Dimbleby, eds.

Folkmar, Daniel. "Social institutions of the Tinglayan Igorot." Unpublished paper at Peabody Library, Harvard University, Manila, 1906.

Forbes, R. J. *Studies in Ancient Technology.* 6 vols. Leiden, 1955–56.

Fortune, Reo. *Manus Religion.* Philadelphia, 1935.

Fourche, J., and Morlighen, H. "Les communications des indigenes du Kasai avec les ames des morts." Institut Royal Colonial Belge, section des sciences morales et politiques, *Memoires,* vol. 9, no. 2. Brussels, 1939.

——. "La danse de Tshishimbi chez les Lulua du Kasai." *Bulletin des seances de l'Institut Royal Colonial Belge* 8, no. 2 (1937).

Frankenberg, Ronald. "Economic anthropology: one anthropologist's view." In Firth, ed.

Frobenius, Leo. *The Voice of Africa.* 2 vols. London, 1913.

Fürer-Haimendorf, Christopher von. *The Konyak Nagas.* New York, 1969.

Gardi, Rene. *Sepik, Land de Sterbenden Geister.* Bern, Switzerland, 1958.

——. *Tambaran.* London, 1960.

Garvan, John M. "Manobos of Mindinao." National Academy of Sciences, *Memoirs,* vol. 23, no. 1. Washington, D.C., 1931.

———. "A survey of the material and sociological culture of the Manobo of eastern Mindinao." *American Anthropologist* 29, no. 4 (1927).

Gerhard, Peter. "Emperor's Dye of the Mixtecs." *Natural History,* January 1964*a.*

———. "Shellfish dye in America." *35th Congreso Internacional de Americanistas. Actas y Memorias,* vol. 3. Mexico, 1964*b.*

Gibson, Harry. "The use of cowries as money during the Shang and Chou periods." *Journal of the North China branch, Royal Asiatic Society,* no. 71 (1941), Shanghai.

Gifford, Edward S. *The Evil Eye: studies in the folklore of vision.* New York, 1958.

Gifford, Edward W. "California shell artifacts." *Anthropological Records* 9, no. 1 (1947), University of California.

———, and Kroeber, A. L. *World Renewal: A Cult System of Native Northwest California.* University of California Press, 1949.

Glasse, R. M., and Meggitt, M. J., eds. *Pigs, Pearlshells and Women: marriage in the New Guinea Highlands.* Englewood Cliffs, N.J., 1969.

Goggin, John M. *Space and Time Perspective in Northern St. Johns Archeology, Florida.* Yale University Publications in Anthropology, no. 47. New Haven, 1952.

Gould, Richard A. "The wealth quest among the Tolowa Indians of northwestern California." *Proceedings of the American Philosophical Society* 110, no. 1 (1966).

———. *Yiwara: foragers of the Australian desert.* New York, 1969.

Greengo, Robert E. "Shellfish foods of the California Indians." *Papers of the Kroeber Anthropological Society,* no. 7 (1952), Berkeley.

Grey, Richard, and Birmingham, David., eds. *Pre-colonial Trade in Africa.* London, 1970.

Griffin, John W. *The Florida Indians and his Neighbors.* Florida, 1949.

Groot, Gerard. *The Prehistory of Japan.* New York, 1951.

———, a. . Sinoto, Yoshihiko. *The Shell Mound of Ubayama.* Nipponica first series, Archaeologia Nipponica, vol. 2. Archaeological Institute of Japan, 1952.

Gulliver, Philip H. *The Family Herds.* London, 1955.

——— and Gulliver, Pamela. "The Central Nilo-Hamites" in *Ethnographic Survey of Africa,* part 7. International African Institute, London, 1953.

Gunther, Erna. *Art in the Life of the Northwest Coast Indians.* Portland Art Museum, Portland, Oregon, 1966.

———. *Indian Life on the Northwest Coast of North America.* Chicago, 1972.

Haberland, von Eike. *Galla Sud-Athiopiens.* Stuttgart, 1963.

Hallpike, Christopher. *The Konso of Ethiopia.* Oxford, 1972.

Halpern, A. M. "A dualism in Pomo cosmology." *Papers of the Kroeber Anthropological Society,* nos. 8–9 (1953), Berkeley.

Harding, J. R. "Conus-shell disc ornaments in Africa." *Man* 62, no. 1 (1962).

Harner, Michael J. *The Jivaro.* New York, 1972.

——— and Essler, Albert B. *Art of the Northwest Coast.* Berkeley, 1965.

Harroy, F. "Ethnographie congolaise. Les Bakubas." *Bulletin de Soc. Royale Belge de Geographie* 31 (Brussels, 1907).

Heizer, Robert F. "Physical analysis of habitation residues." *The Application of Quantitative Methods in Archeology,* edited by R. F. Heizer and S. F. Cook. Viking Fund Publication in Anthropology, no. 28. Berkeley, 1960.

———; Whipple, M. A. *The California Indians.* University of California, 1951.

Herskovits, Melville J. *Dahomey: an ancient west African kingdom.* 2 vols. New York, 1938.

———. *Economic Anthropology: a study of comparative economics.* New York, 1952.

Hildburgh, W. L. "Cowrie shells as amulets in Europe." *Folklore* 53, no. 4 (1942).

———. "Notes on some Tibetan and Bhutia amulets and folk-medicines." *Journal of the Royal Anthropological Institute* 39 (1909).

Hiskett, M. "Materials relating to the cowry currency of the Western Sudan." *Bulletin of the School of Oriental and African Studies* 29, part 2 (1966).

Ho Ting-Jui. "Clothing and ornaments related to Atayal Headhunting." *Taipei University Bulletin,* no. 2 (1953).

———. "Specimens related to Atayal head-hunting ceremonies." *Bulletin of the Department of Archeology and Anthropology,* Taiwan University, no. 4 (1954).

Hocart, A. M. "Lau Islands, Fiji." *Bulletin of the Bernice P. Bishop Museum,* no. 62 (1929), Honolulu.

———. "Canoe and bonito in Eddystone Island." *Journal of the Royal Anthropological Institute* 65 (1935).

———. "The Cult of the Dead in Eddystone of the Solomons." *Journal of the Royal Anthropological Institute* 52 (1922).

Hodson, T. C. "Head-hunting among the hill tribes of Assam." *Folkore* 20, no. 2 (1909).

Hornell, James. *Fishing in Many Waters.* Cambridge University Press, 1950.

———. *The Indian Conch and Its Relation to Hindu Life and Religion.* Marine Zoology of Okhamandal in Kattiawar, vol. 2. London, 1916.

———. "Indian Chank in folklore and religion." *Folklore* 53, no. 2 (1942).

Hudson, G. F. *Europe and China: Survey of their relations from earliest times to 1800.* London, 1931.

Hughes, Ian. "Recent neolithic trade in New Guinea. The ecological basis of traffic in goods among stone-age subsistence farmers." Unpublished Ph.D. dissertation, Australian National University, Canberra, 1971.

Huntingford, G. W. B. *The Galla of Ethiopia.* International African Institute, London, 1955.

Hutton, J. H. *The Angami Nagas.* London, 1921.

Imperato, Pascal James. "Last dances of the Bambara," *Natural History,* April 1975.

im Thurn, Everard. *Among the Indians of Guiana.* London, 1883.

Jackson, J. Wilfred. *Shells as Evidence of the Migrations of Early Culture.* Manchester, 1917.

Jenks, Albert Ernest. *The Bontoc Igorot.* Dept. of Interior, Ethnological Survey Publications, vol. 1. Manila, 1905.

Jennings, John. "Notes on the exhibition of an ethnological collection from Santa Cruz and the New Hebrides." *Journal of the Royal Anthropological Institute,* nos. 1–2 (1898).

Johnson, Marion. "The cowrie currencies of West Africa." *Journal of African History* 11, no. 1 (1970).

Jones, Schuyler. *Men of Influence in Nuristan.* London, 1974.

Kaberry, Phyllis M. *Aboriginal Woman.* London, 1939.

Karsten, Rafael. *The Head-hunters of Western Amazonas.* Societas scientiarum fennica. Commentationes humanarum litterarum, 7, no. 7. Helsingfors, 1935.

Kidder, J. E. *Japan Before Buddhism.* New York, 1959.

Kleiweg de Zwaan, Johannes P. "Houten lampjes van Bali en Oost-Lombok." *Cultureet indie,* vol. 4. Amsterdam, 1942.

Knight, Edward H. "A study of the savage weapons at the centennial exhibition." *Annual Report of the Smithsonian Institution for 1879*, published 1880.

Koike, Hiroko. "Daily growth line of the clam, *Meretrix lusoria:* a basic study for the estimation of prehistoric seasonal gathering." *Journal of the Anthropological Society of Nippon* 81, no. 2 (1973), Tokyo. (Cataloged in AMNH library under *Jinruigaku Zasshi.*)

Koulaseli (also known as Pere Michel Convers). "La corne dans le rituel baoule." *Musees de Geneve*, March 1975.

Kroeber, Alfred L. *Handbook of the Indians of California. Bureau of American Ethnology Bulletin*, no. 78 (1925), Washington, D.C.

————. *Peoples of the Philippines.* American Museum of Natural History Handbook, no. 8. New York, 1928.

Kubler, George. *The Iconography of the Art of Teotihuacan.* Studies in Pre-Columbian Art and Archaeology, no. 4. Dumbarton Oaks, Washington, 1967.

Lacouperie, Terrien de. "The metallic cowries of ancient China (600 B.C.)." *Journal of the Royal Asiatic Society* 20 (1888).

Laguna, Frederica de. *Under Mount Saint Elias: the history and culture of the Yakutat Tlingit.* Smithsonian Contributions to Anthropology, vol. 7. Washington, D.C., 1972.

Lambrecht, Francis. "Ifugao Tales." *Asian Folklore Studies*, vol. 14. Tokyo, 1955.

Lane, Edward W. *An Account of the Manners and Customs of the Modern Egyptians.* London, 1860.

Lane, Frank W. *Kingdom of the Octopus.* London, 1957.

Lange, Charles. *Cochiti; a New Mexico Pueblo.* Austin, Tex., 1959.

Larsson, Karl Erik. "Fijian Studies." *Ethnologiska Studier* 25 (1960), Göteborg.

Lathrap, Donald. *Ancient Ecuador: culture, clay and creativity.* 3000–300 B.C. Field Museum of Natural History. Chicago, 1975.

————. "The antiquity and importance of long distance trade relationships in the moist tropics of pre-Columbian South America." *World Archaeology* 5, no. 2 (1973).

Laxson, D. D. "Strombus lip shell tools of the Tequesta Sub-area." *Florida Anthropology*, vol. 17, no. 4. Tallahassee, 1964.

Laszlo, Andreas. *Doctors, Drums and Dances.* New York, 1955.

Leach, Edmund. " 'Kachin' and 'Haka Chin': a rejoinder to Levi-Strauss." *Man* 4, no. 2 (1969).

Lehman, F. K. *Structure of Chin Society.* Illinois Studies in Anthropology, no. 3. Urbana, 1963.

Lewis, Herbert S. "Neighbors, friends and kinsmen: principles of social organization among the Cushitic-speaking peoples of Ethiopia." *Ethnology* 13, no. 2. (1974).

Li Yih-yuan. "A study of the people of 'tcimo' in the western Paiwan tribe." Academia Sinica, *Taipei Institute of Ethnology, Bulletin*, no. 1 (1956).

Livingstone, David. *Missionary Travels and Researches in South Africa.* New York, 1858.

Loeb, E. M. "Pomo Folkways." *University of California Publications in American Archaeology and Ethnology*, vol. 19. Berkeley, 1926.

Lubbock, John. *Prehistoric Times.* 7th ed. London, 1913.

Lucas, J. Olumide. *The Religion of the Yorubas.* Lagos, Nigeria, 1948.

Lumholtz, Carl. *Symbolism of the Huichol Indians.* American Museum of Natural History Memoirs, vol. 3, part 1. New York, 1900.

Mabuchi, Toichi. "The aboriginal peoples of Formosa." In *Social Structure of Southeast Asia*, edited by G. P. Murdock, Viking Fund Publication in Anthropology, no. 29. New York, 1960.

Mackay, George L. *From Far Formosa.* 3rd ed. Boston, 1898.

Mails, Thomas E. *The Mystic Warriors of the Plains.* New York, 1972.

Malinowski, Bronislaw. *Argonauts of the Western Pacific.* New York, 1922.

Maloney, Clarence, ed. *The Evil Eye.* New York, 1976.

Matson, Frederick R. "Ceramic technology as an aid to cultural interpretation." In *Essays on Archaeological Methods*, edited by James Griffin. Anthropological Papers, Museum of Anthropology, University of Michigan, no. 8. Ann Arbor, 1951.

Mauss, Marcel. *The Gift.* Translated by Ian Cunnison. London, 1954.

McGovern, Janet B. *Among the Head-hunters of Formosa.* Boston, 1922.

McGuire, Joseph D. "A study of the primitive methods of drilling." *Annual Report of the U.S. National Museum for 1894*, published 1896.

Mead, Margaret. *Kinship in the Admiralty Islands.* Anthropological Papers of the American Museum of Natural History, vol. 34, part 2. New York, 1934.

————. *The Mountain Arapesh.* Anthropological Papers of the American Museum of Natural History, vol. 36 (1938), part 1; vol. 37 (1940), part 2.

————. *Sex and Temperament in Three Primitive Societies.* New York, 1935.

Meggitt, Mervyn J. " 'Pigs are our hearts!' The Te exchange cycle among the Mae Enga of New Guinea." *Oceania* 44, no. 3 (1974).

Meighen, Clement W. "Molluscs as food remains in archaeological sites." *Science in Archaeology*, edited by D. Brothwell and E. Higgs. New York, 1970.

————; Pendergast, D. M.; Swartz, B. K.; and Wissler, M. D. "Ecological interpretation in archaeology." *American Antiquity* 24 (1958).

Melitz, Jacques. "Polanyi school of anthropology on money: an economist's view." *American Anthropologist* 72, no. 5 (1970).

Michels, Joseph W. *Dating Methods in Archeology.* New York, 1973.

Miller, Arthur G. *The Mural Painting of Teotihuacan.* Dumbarton Oaks, Washington, D.C., 1973.

Minnich, Helen B. *Japanese Costume.* Rutland, Vt., 1963.

Miracle, M. P. "Plateau Tonga entrepreneurs in historical inter-regional trade." *Rhodes-Livingstone Institute Journal*, no. 26 (1959), Lusaka, Zambia (formerly Northern Rhodesia).

Moore, Clarence B. "Notes on shell implements from Florida." *American Anthropology* 23, no. 1 (1921).

Morse, Edward. "Shell mounds of Omori." *Memoirs of the Science Dept., University of Tokyo*, vol. 1, part 1. Tokyo, 1879.

Morton-Williams, Peter. "The influence of habitat and trade on the politics of Oyo and Ashanti." *Man in Africa*, edited by Mary Douglas and Phyllis Kaberry. London, 1969.

————. "An outline of the cosmology and cult organization of the Oyo Yoruba." *Africa* 34, no. 3 (1964).

Murra, John V. "El trafico de *mullu* en la costa del Pacifico." Paper read at the Primer Simposio de Correlaciones Anthropologicas Andino-Meso-americano. Salinas, Ecuador, 1971.

Murray, Margaret A. "The cowrie shell in Formosa." *Man* 40, no. 1 (1940).

Needham, Rodney. "Percussion and Transition." *Man*, n.s., 2, no. 4 (1967).

Neumann, Franke J. "The flayed god and his rattle-stick: a shamanic element in pre-hispanic Mesoamerican religion." *History of Religions*, vol. 15, no. 3, 1976.

Newton, Douglas. *New Guinea Art in the Collection of the Museum of Primitive Art.* New York, 1967.

Niblack, Albert P. "The coast Indians of southern Alaska and northern British Columbia." *Annual Report of the U.S. National Museum for 1888,* published 1890.

Nuttall, Zelia. "A curious survival in Mexico for the use of Purpura shellfish for dyeing." In *Putnam Anniversary Volume.* Cedar Rapids, Iowa, 1909.

Ojo, G. J. Afolabi. *Yoruba Culture: A Geographical Analysis.* London, 1966.

Olson, Eleanor. *Catalogue of the Tibetan Collection and other Lamaist articles in the Newark Museum,* 2 parts. Newark, 1950.

———. "A Tibetan Buddhist Altar." *The Museum* (new series), vol. 24, no. 4. Newark, 1972.

Parry, N. E. *The Lakhers.* London, 1932.

Parsons, Elsie Clews. *Hopi and Zuni Ceremonialism.* Memoirs of the American Anthropological Association, no. 39. 1933.

———. *Pueblo Indian Religion.* 2 vols. Chicago, 1939.

———. *Social Organization of the Tewa of New Mexico.* Memoirs of the American Anthropological Association, no. 36. 1929.

———. "War god shrines of Laguna and Zuni." *American Anthropologist* 20 (1918).

Paulsen, Allison C. "The Thorny Oyster and the voice of god: Spondylus and Strombus in Andean prehistory." *American Antiquity* 39, no. 4 (1974).

Pearson, Richard. *Archeology of the Ryukyu Islands.* University of Hawaii, Honolulu, 1969.

Pellew, C. "Tyrian Purple." Lecture given at the Metropolitan Museum of Art, reprinted in *Color Trade Journal,* 1918.

Polanyi, Karl. "The economy as instituted process." *Economic Anthropology.* E. E. LeClair and H. K. Schneider, eds., New York, 1968.

Posnansky, Merrick. "Aspects of early West African trade." *World Archaeology* 5, no. 2 (1973).

Poulsen, Jens. "Shell artifacts in Oceania: their distribution and significance." *Pacific Anthropological Records,* no. 11. Bernice P. Bishop Museum, Honolulu, 1970.

Prufer, Olaf. *The McGraw Site: A Study in Hopewellian Dynamics.* Scientific Publication, vol. 4, Cleveland Museum of Natural History, 1965.

Quain, Buell H. *Fijian Village.* Chicago, 1948.

Quentric, Martine. "Notes sur les coutumes vestimentaires des Kalash du Pakistan." *Objets et Mondes* 13 (1973), Musee de l'Homme, Paris.

Quiggin, A. H. *A Survey of Primitive Money.* London, 1949.

Radcliffe-Brown, A. R. *The Andaman Islanders.* Cambridge University Press, 1922.

Rajput, A. B. "Le monde perdu des Kalash (Kafiristan)." *Objets et Monde* 4 (1964), Musee de l'Homme, Paris.

Rappoport, Roy. *Pigs for the Ancestors: Ritual in the ecology of a New Guinea people.* New Haven, 1967.

Rau, Charles. "The archaeological collections of the U.S. National Museum." *Smithsonian Institution Contributions to Knowledge,* vol. 22. Washington, D.C., 1876.

Reichel-Dolmatoff, Gerardo. *Amazonian Cosmos.* Chicago, 1971.

Reischauer, Robert Karl. *Early Japanese History.* 2 vols. Princeton, 1937.

Reynolds, Barrie. *Magic, Divination and Witchcraft among the Barotse of Northern Rhodesia.* Berkeley, 1963.

Richards, A. I. *Chisungu; a girls' initiation ceremony among the Bemba of Northern Rhodesia.* New York, 1956.

Rockhill, W. W. *The Land of the Lamas.* New York, 1891.

Rogers, D. B. "Prehistoric man of the Santa Barbara coast." *Santa Barbara Museum of Natural History,* vol. 1, 1929.

Roosen-Runge, Heinz. "Farbgebung und Tecnik Fruemittelaterlilher Bugmaleri." Studien zu den traktaten "Mappae Clavicula" und "Meraclius," vol. 2. Munich, 1967.

——— and Werner, A. E. A. In *Lindisfarne Gospels.* British Museum, London, 1923.

Ross, Harold. *Baegu: Social and ecological organization in Malaita, Solomon Islands.* Illinois Studies in Anthropology, no. 8. Urbana, 1973.

Roth, Walter E. "An introductory study of the arts, crafts, and customs of the Guiana Indians." *Annual Report of the Bureau of American Ethnology for 1916–17,* published 1924.

Rougier, Emmanuel. "Fijian dances and games." *Transactions of the Fijian Society.* Suva, Fiji, 1915.

Rouse, Irving. "Areas and periods of culture in the Greater Antilles." *Southwest Journal of Anthropology* 7 (1951).

Rubens, Alfred. *A History of Jewish Costume.* New York, 1967.

Ruey Yih-fu. "Ethnographical investigation of some aspects of the Atayal." *Bulletin of the Department of Archeology and Anthropology,* no. 5 (1955), Taiwan University.

Sahlins, Marshall D. "On the sociology of primitive exchange." *The Relevance of Models for Social Anthropology.* Association of Social Anthropologists Monograph, no. 1, Michael Banton, ed. New York, 1965.

Salisbury, Richard F. "Economic anthropology." *Annual Review of Anthropology II,* edited by B. J. Siegal, A. R. Beals, and S. A. Tyler. Palo Alto, Cal., 1973.

———. *Vunamuni; economic transformation in a traditional society.* University of California Press, 1970.

Saltzman, Max; Keay, A. M.; and Christensen, Jack. "The identification of colorants in ancient textiles." *Dyestuffs* 44, no. 8 (New York, 1963). National Aniline Division, Allied Chemical Co.

Schunk, Edward. "Notes on the purple of the ancients." *Journal of the Chemical Society* 35 (1880).

Scott, William Henry. "Economic and material culture of the Kalingas of Madukayan." *Southwest Journal of Anthropology* 14 (1958).

Sejourne, Laurette. *Burning Water; Thought and religion in ancient Mexico.* London, 1956.

———. *El Universo de Quetzalcoatl.* Mexico City, 1962.

Shackleton, N. J. "Marine mollusca in archeology." *Science in Archaeology.* Brothwell, D., and Higgs, E., eds. New York, 1970.

Shepard, Anna O. *Ceramics for the Archaeologist.* Carnegie Institute of Washington Publication 609 (1956).

Silverberg, Robert. *Mound Builders of Ancient America.* Greenwich, Conn., 1968.

Simoni, S. "The Aztecs." In *World Mythology,* edited by Pierre Grimal. London, 1965.

Singer, Charles; Holmyard, E. J.; and Hall, A. R., eds. *A History of Technology.* 2 vols. Oxford, 1956–58.

Skinner, E. P. "Trade and Markets among the Mossi people." In Bohannon and Dalton, eds.

Smith, Cyril S., and Hawthorne, John. "Mappa Clavicula, a little key to the world of medieval techniques." *Transactions of the American Philosophical Society,* vol. 64, part 4. Philadelphia, 1974.

Smith, E. W., and Dale, A. M. *The Ila-speaking Peoples of Northern Rhodesia.*

London, 1920.

Snyderman, George S. "The functions of wampum." *Proceedings of the American Philosophical Society,* vol. 98. Philadelphia, 1954.

Soustelle, Jacques. *The Four Suns.* Translated by E. Ross. London, 1971.

Sparks, B. W. "Non-marine mollusca and archaeology." *Science in Archeology.* Brothwell, D., and Higgs, E., eds. New York, 1970.

Speck, Frank G. "The functions of wampum among the eastern Algonkin." *Memoirs of the American Anthropological Association,* no. 6. 1919.

Speiser, Feilx. *Ethnographische Materialen aus den Neuen Hebriden und den Banks-Inseln.* Berlin, 1923.

Spooner, Brian. "The Evil Eye in the Middle East." In *Witchcraft, Confessions and Accusations,* Association of Social Anthropologists Monograph, no. 9, edited by Mary M. Douglas. London, 1970.

Starr, Frederick. *Congo Natives: an ethnographic album.* Chicago, 1912.

Stearns, R. E. C. "Ethno-conchology; a study of primitive money." *Report of the U.S. National Museum,* 1887.

Stephen, Alexander M. *Hopi Journal.* Edited by Elsie C. Parsons. Columbia University Contributions to Anthropology, vol. 23, parts 1–2. New York, 1936.

Stevenson, Matilda C. "The Sia." *Annual Report of the Bureau of American Ethnology for 1889–90,* published 1894.

———. "Zuni Indians." *Annual Report of the Bureau of American Ethnology for 1901–2,* published 1904.

Strabo. *The Geography of Strabo.* Translated by H. C. Hamilton and W. Falconer. Bohn's Classical Library, London, 1906.

Strathern, Andrew. *The Rope of Moka: Big Men and ceremonial exchange in Mount Hagen, New Guinea.* Cambridge University Press, 1971.

——— and Strathern, Marilyn. *Self-Decoration in Mount Hagen.* London, 1974.

Strathern, Marilyn. *Women in Between: Female roles in a male world: Mount Hagen, New Guinea.* New York, 1972.

Swann, Nancy Lee (translator and annotator). *Food and Money in Ancient China.* Princeton, 1950.

Tannahill, Reay. *Food in History.* New York, 1973.

Thompson, J. E. S. *Maya Hieroglyphic Writing.* 2d ed. Civilization of the American Indian, no. 56. University of Oklahoma Press, 1960.

Thompson, Laura. "Southern Lau; Fijian ethnography." *Bulletin of the Bernice P. Bishop Museum,* no. 162 (1940), Honolulu.

Thompson, Robert Farris. "An aesthetic of the cool." *African Arts,* 7, no. 1 (1973).

———. *Black Gods and Kings; Yoruba Art at UCLA.* Bloomington, Ind. (1976).

Tindale, Norman B. *Aboriginal Tribes of Australia.* Berkeley, 1974.

Torday, Emil. *On the Trail of the Bushongo.* London, 1925.

——— and Joyce, T. A. "Notes ethnographiques sur les peuples communement applés Bakuba." *Annales du Musee du Congo Belge,* Anthropologie Serie III. Brussels, 1910.

Tower, Donald B. "The use of marine mollusca and their value in reconstructing prehistoric trade routes in the American Southwest." *Papers of the Excavators' Club,* vol. 2, no. 3. Cambridge, Mass., 1945.

Uberoi, J. Singh. *Politics of the Kula Ring.* Manchester University Press, 1962.

Ucko, Peter, and Dimbleby, G. W., eds. *The domestication and exploitation of Plants and Animals.* London, 1969.

Underhill, Ruth M. *Papago Indian Religion.* New York, 1946.

Vanoverbergh, Morice. "Dress and adornment in the mountain province of Luzon, Philippine Islands." *Publications of the Catholic Anthropological Conference,* vol. 1. Washington, D.C., 1929.

Vansina, Jan. "Les croyances religieuses des Kuba." *Zaire* 12, no. 7 (1958), Brussels.

———. "Initiation rituals of the Bushong." *Africa* 25 (1955).

———. "Miko mi Yool, une association religieuse Kuba." *Aequatoria* 12, nos. 2–3 (1959), Coquilhatville, Belgian Congo.

———. "Le royaume Kuba." *Annales du Musee Royal de l'Afrique Centrale,* Series 8, Sciences Humaines, no. 49. Tervuren, Belgium, 1964.

———. "Trade and markets among the Kuba." In Bohannon and Dalton, 1962.

Verger, Pierre. "Notes sur le culte des *Orisa* et *Vodun* a Bahia." *Memoires,* no. 51. Institut Francais d'Afrique Noire, Dakar, 1957.

Wang Yu Ch'uan. *Early Chinese Coinage.* American Numismatic Society Monograph, no. 122. New York, 1951.

Webster, William J. "A new concept for the Busycon shell receptacle." *Florida Anthropologist* 23, no. 1 (1970), Orlando.

Wei Hwei-lin. "Investigation of social organization of the Chal'abus Paiwan." *Bulletin of the Department of Archeology and Anthropology,* no. 5 (1955), Taiwan University.

———. "Supplementary notes on the Formosan aborigines." *Social Structure in Southeast Asia,* G. Murdock, ed. Viking Fund Publication in Anthropology, vol. 29. New York, 1960.

Weide, Margaret. "Seasonality of Pismo clam collecting." *Annual Report Archeological Survey,* vol. 2. Anthropology Dept., UCLA, 1969.

Wescott, Joan. "The sculpture and myths of Eshu-Elegba, the Yoruba trickster." *Africa* 32, no. 4 (1962).

——— and Morton-Williams, Peter. "The symbolism and ritual context of the Yoruba Laba Shango." *Journal of the Royal Anthropological Institute* 92, no. 1 (1962).

West, George. "Tobacco, pipes and smoking customs of the American Indians." *Bulletin* of the Public Museum of Milwaukee 17. 1934.

Westheim, Paul. *The Art of Ancient Mexico.* New York, 1965.

Willett, Frank. *African Art.* New York, 1971.

Williams, Francis Edgar. *Papuans of the Trans-Fly.* Anthropology Report, Territory of Papua, no. 15. Oxford, 1936.

Winters, Howard D. "Value systems and trade cycles of the Late Archaic in the Midwest." In Binford and Binford, eds.

Wissler, Clark. "Ceremonial bundles of the Blackfoot Indians." *Anthropological Papers of the American Museum of Natural History,* vol. 7. New York, 1912.

Wood, William. *New England's Prospect.* 1634. Reprint. West Newbury, Mass., 1898.

Woodward, Arthur. "A modern Zuni pilgrimage." *Masterkey* 6, no. 2 (1932), Los Angeles.

Wooley, C. L. *Ur Excavations: The Royal Cemetery.* 2 vols. University of Pennsylvania, 1934.

Worcester, Dean C. "The non-Christian tribes of northern Luzon." *Philippine Journal of Science* 1, no. 8 (1906), Manila.

Zamora, Mario D. *Studies in Philippine Anthropology (in honor of H. Otley Beyer).* Quezon City, Philippines, 1967.

Photographic Sources and Credits

The source of each photograph is listed first, followed by dimensions in the case of artifacts. Frances McLaughlin Gill is listed as FMG and the American Museum of Natural History as AMNH. When photographs have been reproduced from books, the pertinent information is given. Other photographs were obtained from the photographers.

Shells in daily life

Page 16: AMNH. Von Luschan Collection. Photographer unknown. Ca. 1900; *page 19:* AMNH. Edward Curtis; *page 23:* AMNH. Case in Hall of Mollusks and Mankind; *page 26:* FMG. Mask: 5″ × 6″ high; *page 28:* FMG. Lime container: approx. 2½″ diameter; *page 29:* Jane Safer, 1967; *page 30:* FMG. Auger: 10½″ high; rasp: 14″ high; *page 31:* AMNH. Leahy/Chinnery Expedition. Ca. 1933; *page 32:* AMNH. J. Kirchner, 1917 (detail); Cutting shell: from Gardi, 1958; *page 33:* From Gardi, 1958; *page 34:* L. Cipriani; *page 37:* FMG. Philippines scoops: 10″ long; 8″ long; *page 38:* FMG. Fishhooks (California, Marshall Islands, Cook Islands, Solomons): approximately 1½″ across (California) to 3½″ long (Marshall Islands); *page 39:* FMG. Scraper: 4½″ high. Knife: 2¼″ diameter. Fiber extractor: 3¼″ high. Tweezers: 1½″ across; *page 40:* FMG. Solomons bowl: 19″ long; *page 41:* FMG. Detail of Solomons bowl; *page 42:* FMG. Detail of Peruvian bowl; *page 44:* FMG. Coca bag: 6″ × 7″. Cushion: 7½″ square; *page 45:* FMG. Detail of coca bag; *page 46:* FMG. Ax: approx. 15″ long; *page 47:* FMG. Octopus lure: approx. 13½″ long; Man with ax: AMNH. Leahy/Chinnery Expedition. Ca. 1933.

Shells as wealth

Page 48: FMG. Detail of Green Snail Shell necklace; *page 51:* AMNH. Leahy/Chinnery Expedition. Ca. 1933; *page 53:* AMNH; *page 54:* AMNH. Wanamaker, 19th century; *page 56:* AMNH. Edward Curtis; *page 59:* Museum of the American Indian, New York City. Frederick Starr; *page 62:* Andrew and Marilyn Strathern; *page 64:* AMNH. Leahy/Chinnery Expedition. Ca. 1933; *page 67:* A. L. Epstein; *page 68:* AMNH; *page 69:* FMG. Bracelet: approx. 2½″ diameter; *page 70:* AMNH. Emmons, 1888; *page 71:* AMNH. Edward Curtis, 1910; *page 73:* FMG. Pipe: approx. 7″ long; *page 74:* FMG. Spondylus necklace: approx. 10″ diameter; *page 75:* FMG. Burmese heirloom: approx. 5½″ long; *page 76:* FMG. Detail of Dentalia shells; *page 77:* FMG. Dentalia: approx. 24″ long. Purse: approx. 5¼″ wide; Shasta woman: AMNH. R. Wanamaker; *page 78:* FMG. Beads: approx. 5″ long. Basket: approx. 7″ diameter; Indian girl: AMNH. Edward Curtis; *page 79:* FMG. Shell money, Rossel Island: 7½″ long. Green Snail Shell: 4″ long. Solomon Islands: 2″ diameter. New Britain: 35″ long; *page 80:* FMG. Green Snail valuables. Single piece: 7″. Waist ornament: each shell about 3½″ high; *page 81:* FMG. Crescent: approx. 9″ diameter; "Big-man": Andrew and Marilyn Strathern; *page 82:* FMG. Detail of shell bib; *page 83:* FMG. Shell bib: 17″ high × 13″ wide.

Shells as emblems of status

Page 84: Detail of kap-kaps; *page 86:* FMG. Turkana belt: 30″ long; *page 87:* Gregory Bateson; *page 89:* Stella Snead; *page 90:* AMNH; *page 91:* AMNH. Detail; *page 92:* From Radcliffe-Brown, 1922; *page 93:* FMG. Skull: Margaret Mead Collection; Artisan painting skull: Gregory Bateson; *page 95:* Tervuren Museum, Belgium. L. Achten; *page 98:* From Lazslo, 1955; *page 99:* From Smith and Dale, 1920; *page 100:* Harold Ross; FMG. Kapkaps: 2½″–4½″ diameter; *page 101:* FMG. Fiji breastplate: 8½″ diameter; *page 102:* Margaret Mead Collection (both photographs); *page 102:* FMG: Canoe prow: approx. 26″ long; *page 104:* From Butler, 1855; *page 105:* From Parry, 1932; *page 106:* From Chen Chi-lu, 1968; *page 107:* AMNH. Jesse Tarbox Beals, 1904; *page 108:* AMNH. Jesse Tarbox Beals, 1904; *page 109:* FMG. Igorot disc: approx. 8″ diameter; *page 110:* FMG. Dance belt: 24″ long; *page 111:* FMG. Detail of dance belt; *page 112:* FMG. Mask: approx. 22″ high; *page 113:* FMG. Mask: 13″ high; *page 114:* FMG. Vahumbe ornament: overall 36″ long; Vahumbe woman: from Lazslo, 1955; *page 115:* FMG. Ornament: approx. 9″ × 6″; Warrior: Margaret Mead Collection; *page 116:* FMG. War shield: approx. 40″ high; *page 117:* FMG. Powder horn: 13½″ long; Lakher man: from Parry, 1932; *page 118:* FMG. Paiwan headdress: approx. 7″ diameter; Taiwan nobleman: from Chen Chi-lu, 1968; *page 119:* FMG. Lime spatula: overall 12″; carving: 6″ high.

Shells in ritual and myth

Page 102: FMG. Detail of Kachina doll; *page 124:* FMG. Pendant: 6½″ long; *page 125:* AMNH. A. Elkin (detail); *page 128:* AMNH. Harold McCormick; *page 129:* FMG. Hunters' fetishes: approx. 7″ long; *page 130:* AMNH. Harold McCormick; *page 132:* AMNH. Wanamaker; *page 134:* From Wescott, 1962; *page 139:* Andrew and Marilyn Strathern; *page 141:* National Media Production Center, Manila, Philippines; *page 142:* AMNH. D. C. Worcester; *page 145:* From M. W. Stirling in *Bureau of American Ethnology Bulletin,* no. 117, 1938, plate 10; *page 146:* AMNH. Winter and Poole, 19th century; *page 147:* AMNH. Godard; *page 149:* From *A World of Islands* by June Knox-Mawer. New York, 1972. Photographs by Peter Carmichael; *page 151:* Stella Snead; *page 152:* British Museum; *page 154:* AMNH; *page 155:* Courtesy Andre Emmerich Gallery; *page 156:* AMNH; *page 157:* FMG. Quetzalcoatl emblem: approx. 3½″ diameter; *page 158:* FMG. Detail of fetish necklace: approx. 26″ long; Man wearing necklace: AMNH. Harold McCormick; *page 159:* FMG. Kachina doll: approx. 12″ high; Kachina dancers: AMNH. Harold McCormick; *page 160:* FMG. Cockle shell pipe: approx. 5½″ wide × 3½″ high; *page 161:* FMG. Borneo rattle: approx. 8″ high; *page 162:* FMG. Fetish figure: approx. 15″ high; *page 163:* FMG. Elegba ornament: longest pendant approx. 14″ long; Priestess: from Wescott, 1962; *page 164:* FMG. Olokun necklace: 24 cm diameter; *page 165:* FMG. Fan: 17 cm high × 8.2 cm wide; *page 166:* FMG. Detail of West African mask: 14″ high (carved wood head only; 22″ with raffia ruff); *page 167:* FMG. West African mask: approx. 16″ wide × 13″ high (excluding pendant nose); FMG. New Guinea mask; *page 168:* FMG. Soundmakers: Philippines tinkler: discs: 2½″–3″ diameter. Trumpet: 9½″ long. Shaman's rattle: 7″ wide × 8″ high. Indian conch: 5″ long; *page 169:* FMG. Jivaro dance belt: 48″ long; 7½″ pendant; Jivaro woman: from Stirling; *page 170:* FMG. Hupa skirt: 32″ including fringe; Yurok girl: from AMNH, Godard; *page 171:* FMG. Detail of shaman's belt: approx. 36″ long; *page 172:* FMG. Philippines bracelets: 2½″–3½″ diameter; Bagobo girl: National Media Production Center, Manila, Philippines; *page 173:* FMG. Funerary stick: overall height: approx. 15″; *page 174:* FMG. Yamabushi trumpet: approx. 15″; *page 175:* From Mawer, 1972; *page 176:* FMG. Detail of Tibetan trumpet; *page 177:* FMG. Tibetan trumpet: overall length 19″ high × 11″ wide; *page 178:* FMG. Mexican trumpet: approx. 14″; *page 179:* FMG. Detail of Mexican trumpet; *page 180:* FMG. Detail of puppet: 12″ high (not including 8″ stick); Chinese puppet: AMNH.

Index